TOO PHASED

A novel By

DAPHNE JACKSON

Too Phased
Copyright @ 2022 by Little Publishing, LLC

All rights reserved. No portion of this book may be reproduced, stored in a retrieval system, or transmitted by any means electronic, mechanical, photocopy recording, scanning, or other except brief quotations without prior written permission of the publisher, except in case of brief quotations embodied in critical reviews and certain other noncommercial uses permitted by copyright law.

For permission requests, write to the publisher, addressed "Attention Permissions Coordinator," at aalittle08@gmail.com

Published By: Little Publishing, LLC
Little Publishing, LLC
aalittle08@gmail.com

Ordering Information:
Quantity Sales: Special discounts are available on quantity purchases by corporations, associations, and nonprofits. For details, contact the publisher at the address above.

ISBN: 978-0-578-39264-6

DEDICATION

Thank God for changing my direction. What keeps me grounded is knowing that I am not alone. I didn't make it this far on my own. This story is full of trials and tribulations that open doors to the healing process. At some point, you can no longer place blame on the people who hurt you for the direction of your life. You can hold them accountable for their part, but you learn that after what's been done, you still must live.

Thank you to my son. You are living proof that love heals.

Often, we try to dissociate from our past to develop the versions of ourselves we want to become, but situations trigger the parts of us that we didn't acknowledge. This is my belief. Life experiences alter how we see the world and how we react. Suffering could either manifest into fear of the unknown or fuel to succeed. That is what I believe, but what I do not believe is that we are destined to be like anyone with which we are connected. No matter how similar the experience, the person makes a difference.

TABLE OF CONTENTS

Introduction 1

Chapter One: May I unpack? 5

Chapter Two: Different Addresses, Different Accesses 15

Chapter Three: Books Before Boys because Boys Make Babies . . 25

Chapter Four: New Addition 35

Chapter Five: Trigger Warning! 43

Chapter Six: Grace 55

Chapter Seven: One of Many 67

Chapter Eight: New Beginnings 79

Chapter Nine: Lessons Learned 93

Chapter Ten: Cycles 105

Chapter Eleven: Fight or Flight 117

About the Author 129

INTRODUCTION

I used to call myself an optimist. I prided myself on seeing the bright side of the difficult times in my life. Even when things were bad, I knew that something good was bound to happen. I would convince myself that I was ok when I knew that I was suffering. I could cry myself to sleep and wake up a warrior. Being an optimist had its pros and cons. I put myself in a lot of compromising situations by constantly thinking of favorable outcomes and trying to find the good in everyone. It was my defense mechanism for survival. Going along to get along caused me a lot of pain. I'm speaking about pain that was internal, that I couldn't put a bandage on the pain that raised me. Some lessons I learned from witnessing other people's outcomes and it vicariously matured me. Those lessons still didn't save me from problems. I believe it is true that you learn more from living than any book or lecture could ever teach. We all say, "When I grow up," with so much enthusiasm and so little awareness of how soon that will be or what may define that. Growing up is not just age. Maturing is experience, exposure, perception, and conflict. Feeling that it is time for a change and doing what is necessary to change doesn't always happen instantaneously.

Growing up, I moved several times. I had so many addresses, most in the same zip code. Twice in the same community. We were not recipients of housing assistance programs, but my mom had her reasons. Some were as simple as the aesthetic of the house. She had to have a basement and two bathrooms without question. The constant changes were bizarre to me because the neighborhoods were similar. Over time I learned that windows, cabinets, fixtures, paint, countertops, appliances, etc., depicted the modernization of the house and, if renting, if your landlord is adherent. I was still able to attend the same schools all but once. Most of my friends stayed the same because of school. Moving was always sentimental for me, but my mom had a way of decorating that made every house comfortable. Even when we lived in the projects, she cleaned and decorated as if we lived in a mansion. She made the hood appear as a luxury stay. My mom kept financial matters private, but I knew when things were bad by her mood.

My mom told me stories of how people were drawn to me at a young age and how I would see pictures on shirts and create stories. She shared with me a story about how she unknowingly sent me to school dressed in another school's uniform. She had purchased the uniform from the thrift store because she liked the colors. By the time our neighbor told her that she saw me at the bus stop dressed in the other school's uniform, I had already gone off to school. My mom said she worried about me and looked forward to me calling home. I was in the 6th grade. She told me that she observed me get off the bus; I was smiling, so happy rocking that uniform that it made her feel good. Her words were, "You were so confident; I couldn't do anything but smile." She shared that story after I had graduated high school, but it meant so much to me at that stage of my life. I had overcome so much. The confidence that my mom spoke of was of my young unconscious mind. I was in the 11th grade when I looked at myself in a new light. I knew what it meant to "Find yourself." I knew that I didn't have everything, but I believed in myself. I knew that I was enough. I knew that I couldn't thrive in my environment.

INTRODUCTION

My mom tried to move away from the hood several times, but we would always end up in the same environments. She would always say she wanted to move far away, but we always made our way back to what was familiar. My grandmother lived in the projects for over 20 years, and we would visit every weekend. It was always a party at my grandmother's house, and everyone in the community was related in some way. My mom always talked about breaking the cycle and encouraged us to be better than her. She became offensive when we spoke out about the way we were treated. She neutralized us by making statements such as, "Mama didn't do shit for me, and I turned out fine." Then, she would go on a rant about how we had food, shelter, and clean clothes. My mom believed in tough love. That doesn't mean that she wasn't affectionate. I did grow up in a home where we openly expressed love. My mom was that aunt in the family who kissed all the nieces and nephews and handed out money at the functions. I felt that she gave her best self to the people on the outside. Sometimes it was like she lived a double life. Being the middle child and the only child without an involved father intensified my attachment to my mother. My perception of her was different from my siblings', but they would say that I was my mother's favorite child. I do not feel that my mom favored any of her children or loved anyone more than the other. I would even say that when my stepfather lived with us, my mom favored my younger brother because his father was present in the household. In our household, the rule was, "What goes on in the house stays in the house."

Chapter One

MAY I UNPACK?

My older sister and I were like night and day, but our relationship was like caramel and chocolate. We didn't attend the same school, and we had different friends. In her earlier years, she was bullied too, but my mom taught her how to fight. One of the girls in our neighborhood took a photo that my sister kept in the front pocket of her binder and threw it in the dumpster. My mom had warned my sister not to take the photo to school, but she wanted to follow the trend. When my sister came home and told my mom, my mom took the mattress off the bed, put it on the floor, and wrestled with her until she learned how to fight. When my sister started fighting back, she became fearless. Ironically, her first fight was to defend me from an older girl I had been hanging out with.

I was still in elementary when my big sister dropped out of school, and she was out of the house at the age of 12. The school administrators had my mom's number on speed dial. I would hear the voicemails that the principal left when she was caught sneaking out of the school. One day, I came home from school and my family was having an intervention with my sister. By the time I had taken my books in my room, my big brother had taken her in the room and whipped her. I was supposed to be cleaning shrimp but hearing my sister cry made me cry. My mom saw me and told me to stay in school so that it wouldn't happen to me.

At first, my sister was the shy and quiet one. I was outgoing and friendly. I had plenty of friends, but my sister preferred to hang out with boys. Over time, my sister began to sneak out of the house and date guys who were older. Eventually, she started sneaking them into the house. I could recall waking up one night and seeing my sister's boyfriend standing over me. When I jumped up, my sister laughed at me. She had snuck him in the side door of our apartment. They were talking in the pitch-black dark room, and all I could see was their teeth. I didn't even know my sister was that bold. My mom had got incarcerated for a traffic violation, and I stayed at my godsister's house for the weekend. When I came back home, my mom was furious. Our apartment was burglarized, and it was rumored that my sister's boyfriend was the culprit. My mom was trying to understand why our apartment was targeted. I told my mom what I had witnessed, and she called the police. She reported him and my sister as his accomplice.

I didn't know that my mom would report my sister too, and when the police arrived, they determined that my sister didn't commit a crime. They also stated that my mom didn't have enough evidence to prove that her boyfriend even burglarized our place. My mom was desperate for justice. She asked my sister to make a statement, but my sister refused to incriminate her boyfriend. She defended his innocence after everyone in the community had already exposed him. That is when my mom plotted me against my sister. She asked me to tell the police that my sister had assaulted her. Tears came down my eyes, and I said no. My mom pleaded with me as she expressed how the situation affected her. She said that my sister would get out, but she needed to learn a lesson. My mom called the police again and told them that my sister had assaulted her. My sister refuted, but when I agreed with my mom, the officer believed us. When the officer put the handcuffs on my sister, she looked at me like I had betrayed her. My mom recovered her television from the guy's friend's house that evening, but I still didn't feel good about lying against my sister. That first arrest led to plenty more.

Chapter One—MAY I UNPACK?

I was in the 6th grade when my mom experienced hard times and moved us to the hood where she had grown up. She had already expressed that we wouldn't be there long. When we moved, I was bullied instantly. First, my older sister's adversary greeted me. I recall walking through the hallway of what was then West Fulton Middle school and having a tall, slim girl tell me that her sister wanted to fight me. I had never met her before, so I was certain that she had approached me in error. A week had passed, and the same girl approached me again and said, "Amber wants to fight you." I acknowledged her that time. "Your sister's name is Amber?" I asked. "Yeah, she said she beat your sister up, and she wants to fight you," she responded. I was eager to interrogate my sister about her and Amber's confrontation because I knew it had to be serious for her to scout me. She had to have seen me in the community to know that my sister and I were siblings.

My older sister was considered a juvenile delinquent. She had been committed to the state and was then placed in a group home. I had to wait until she called me, so I tried my best to avoid Amber's sister. Eventually, my sister called, and she enlightened me about her altercation with Amber. My sister, like most big sisters, was protective of me. Amber carried a grudge for months over a simple fight and targeted me to get payback. When I told my sister that I had never seen Amber, she described her to me and assured me that she would take care of it on her visit home. I finally saw Amber with her two sisters, and I immediately thought of the "Gross sisters" from the Proud Family. The messenger, the one who alerted me for Amber, was the tall sister. Then, there was the other sister, who was a bit shorter. She looked younger than me, so I eliminated the thought of her being Amber. Then, I spotted Amber. I examined her physique and appearance. She was barely 5 feet tall. She was taut, cocoa complexioned, and had a solid physique. She had calves like she ran track. Her jacket was hung off her shoulders, and she had her hand up to her mouth, with her sleeves covering her hand. She even wore old Reeboks just like my sister described. I was intimidated. I watched them walk home, and I walked in the opposite direction.

One day, Amber saw me walking by myself on the school steps and pushed me. I turned around and stared at her in her eyes and walked to the opposite side of the steps. I went home and told my mom about my encounter with Amber. She wasn't aware that I had been experiencing bullying or that I had been communicating with my sister. My mom wanted to put an end to it, so we walked to Amber's house that evening. There were a lot of children in their apartment, but Amber and her mom weren't there. As we were walking back home, Amber, her mom, and more people were approaching us. My mom stopped them and introduced herself. She began to explain the purpose of our meeting. I noticed that the family had formed a circle around me and my mom. I don't think that it was intentional, but my mom recognized it too and changed her tone. She made it known that our meeting was for the purpose of peace. My mom went on to inform Amber's mom that I attended school to learn and that my sister and I were totally different. Amber's mom was pleasant to us, and she was just as appalled as my mom after hearing about her daughter bullying me. She chastised Amber right in front of us and ordered her to apologize to me. Amber's sisters and I even became cool after that, but the bullying from others had just begun. I guess it was just a new girl on the block treatment.

I was bullied for my size, my hair, and because I was alone. I also wore glasses. I fit the description of a conventional nerd. Most people had siblings or family with who they formed cliques, but I wasn't accepted yet. The friends that I did have didn't want to be included. I remember the first time I was bullied about my hair. I

Chapter One—MAY I UNPACK?

wore a sleek, high faux curly ponytail. I was walking down the hallway by myself, and a clique of boys and girls were behind me. Suddenly, I felt someone pull my hair, and the ponytail fell off. Everyone started laughing. I grabbed the ponytail from the floor, went into the restroom, and fixed my hair. I overheard the girl who pulled my hair say, "I told y'all that wasn't her hair." I remember crying in the bathroom before I went back to class. I couldn't allow them to see me sad, and I never told my mom about it because I didn't want her to worry about me.

Our science teacher didn't have control over any of her classes. The books were damaged, but she still gave us work to do in the book. Very few people completed the assignments. When the class would get off task, she could never redirect us because no one listened. I can recall a time when I was just standing, observing some of my classmates making up rhymes and joking with each other in science class. The chorus was "__ __got it, what he/she got, it rhymes with__, a __." I saw the girl look at me, and I knew she would come for me. Her rhyme was "Adore got it, what she got, it rhymes with hot, a big ass bald spot." I laughed to lessen some of the humiliation. I had a permanent scar from a 3rd degree burn on the right side of my head. My mom tried to cover the scars on my head with certain hairstyles, and I wouldn't wear certain styles for many years because I didn't want it to show. I had a rhyme in mind that I wanted to say so bad, but I just didn't feel safe because she was popular, and I felt alone. "__got it, what she got, it rhymes with city, some musty titties," I laughed to myself. I knew that her friends would agree that she was musty too, but I didn't know how she would respond to the same type of embarrassment she inflicted on me.

The truth was that I wasn't alone. I wasn't timid either. I certainly didn't lack wits. That wasn't even my first time living in the hood. The bullying stopped when it was discovered that my family was well known in the community. Some of our parents grew up together and were still cool. I became friends with most of the "bullies" just because our community was so closely knit. Everyone was basically cousins. I even discovered my brother on my father's side. After that incident happened, I wanted it to be known that I wasn't afraid but outnumbered. Whenever I heard an insult, I clapped back. I walked taller with my head high, and I made myself seen within my studies, especially when it was time to read aloud. People would try to use me to copy my work or cheat on tests, but when they didn't need me, the jokes continued.

I had been introduced to my brother on my dad's side when I first moved into the neighborhood. Our mothers were cool and respected one another. Our dad wasn't active in either of our lives, but that didn't help the division between us. When we were introduced to one another, my brother didn't take a liking to me because of my status at school. My brother was popular, and he told me that I needed to defend myself. I informed him that I wasn't just going to punch someone in the face for talking about me and he said that I should. He treated me like everyone else. I got into my first fight at school, outside of the gym. I will never forget that fight because it taught me so much. That wasn't my first fight in my life, but the first one where I felt like a small fish in a tank full of sharks.

I was in the gym for physical education class when I decided to go play volleyball with a girl who had been throwing a volleyball in the air. I asked her if I could play with her, and she consented. She gave me the ball, and I served first. She hit the ball so hard that it got stuck in the ceiling. As I headed back to the bleachers to collect my things, I passed up one of my peers. I pointed to the ball in the ceiling and made a joke about the girl who served it. I heard

Chapter One—MAY I UNPACK?

everyone cheering that it was about to be a fight by the time I approached the gym exit. When I got outside, my friends were all prep talking to me like before a boxer entered a boxing ring.

Sonya Evans: "You called me a bitch?"

"No, but what's up," I replied. Sonya's jacket was already off and hanging on the rail, so I knew we were past talking at that point. I asked two of my friends to grab me if they saw an adult. I swung at her first, and she grabbed my hood over my head. I was swinging so fast that I backed her into the rail. She tripped, and we fell to the ground. The principal was approaching, and I was still on top of her. My friends were grabbing me, and I slightly heard them calling my name, but I was too in the moment. Once I snapped out of it, everyone was commending me, and my friends said never to ask them to save me again. People were patting me and smiling in approval like I had won a black belt. The principal approached us and asked who was in a fight. I couldn't believe Sonya spoke up and she didn't even get caught. I rolled my eyes at Sonya and walked alongside the principal on the opposite side of Sonya. The principal chose to speak with Sonya first and came to get me out of class later. Sonya took full responsibility and admitted to being the aggressor due to peer pressure. She saved us both from suspension. We had to apologize to one another and received a lecture about peer pressure. We left with a warning. I never did understand why it was so important that I could fight before people wanted to be my friend. I knew plenty of people who I had never witnessed be in a fight. I wondered what it was about them that magnetized respect.

By the 7th grade, I had real friends. I wouldn't consider myself popular, but I was well known. Eventually, I gravitated towards people who liked me for me. Being popular was never a goal for me. I enjoyed school because I liked to learn. Among my genuine friends during that time was a girl named Jade. She was always very quiet, unlike me, who always raised my hand in class to speak or read. We didn't take every class together because we were divided into small learning communities according to our academic standing. We did have one class together where we would talk and do our work together. I guess I brought attention to Jade because our teacher kept calling her out about her class participation and "just enough to get by" grades. Jade was kind and kept an unbothered demeanor. She was more observant than talkative, and her tolerance was low for pettiness. She spoke up when people were disruptive in class. She was only 4 feet tall and tiny, but everyone respected her. She also boxed at the community center and was cool with a lot of guys. I didn't know why she gravitated to me, but I liked her because she was genuine.

My father reappeared in my life when he visited a local bar that my family happened to be attending as well. My older cousin spotted him and made it her business to reunite us. When she noticed him, she immediately came to my mom's house, where I was hanging out with my friend. I dressed swiftly and asked my friend to come with me. It was late, around 8 pm. The bar was within walking distance from the community. We all walked to the bar along with another friend who saw us walking. When we arrived in the parking lot, my cousin asked about my dad and some men disclosed that we'd just missed him as he had just left for the store. My friends and I sat on a random truck and waited while my cousin conversed with the men.

A man approached the car and said, "I know which one is mine." "You," he said, greeting me with a hug. His face looked just like mine. He had Chubby cheeks, caramel skin tone, and he smelled like expensive cologne. I couldn't help but feel good about seeing him. I felt so complete. That was the second time I had ever seen my father. I remember meeting my dad once when I was around three years old, but my mom told me he had died. I was 12 years old. My uncle was listening to our conversation close by and imparted that I was sneaky. I just said, "OK." I didn't consider myself a sneaky person, but I didn't want to go into detail with him in the parking lot. My father and I exchanged numbers, and he reached in his pocket and gave me all of the $40s. I didn't even care about the money. That moment was so sentimental to me. I felt on top of the world.

Things turned sour on Monday. I arrived at school and gossip was traveling around that my brother shared that my dad disclaimed me. Everything with us had been going so well. He had just started acknowledging me as his sister and it felt like we had formed a relationship. I walked down the hallway, and everyone was hanging around, talking with friends until the bell rang. Teachers were yelling down the halls to move the crowd and congregate students into the classrooms. Everything seemed normal until I walked right into an ambush. I didn't even get my foot in the door when I heard my brother's voice, "Hell nah, my daddy said she is not his child." My brother was sitting down in my English class surrounded by other students. I walked in and took a seat. My heart sunk to my feet. My dad wasn't present in his life either, but there he was proudly calling him dad and belittling me. The bell rang abruptly, and my brother hopped from the desk and sprinted across the hall to his class. The whole day I couldn't focus on anything. I just wanted to be invisible and cry. I got on the school bus that afternoon and laid my head on the windowpane, replaying the encounter with my dad repeatedly. When the bus stopped, I released my tears and power-walked home. I called my mom's name as soon as I opened the front door. She was rinsing dye from her hair. I sat on her bed crying as she reached for a towel and dried her face. My mom asked what happened, and I struggled to get the words out.

"He said… he told my brother and his mom that I wasn't his child," I cried. "Everyone knows about it," I added. My mom looked over at me and said, "He's a damn lie; he knows that you are his child; We took a test & he knows you look just like them folks."

Emotionally Wrecked is an understatement. I felt betrayed, abandoned, and unloved. Why would he say that? Why would he pretend to care about me? My mom called my dad and told him that I came home from school crying from something I heard at school. She did not disclose anything else but instead gave me the phone. He spoke very softly, with concern in his voice. He asked me what was said, but I couldn't articulate words through the tears. He interfered, "I can imagine what was said, and it is not true." He continued, "I made some mistakes, but I want to fix them." He asked me to wipe my tears. Then, he asked me what I wanted for Christmas. I smiled and put my hand over the phone so he could not hear me ask my mom what I needed. Then, I swiftly moved my hand and mentioned to him that I wanted a computer. "A desktop or a laptop?" He asked. My mom and I echoed, "desktop!" When we hung up, my mom gave me a prep talk. She told me something that stuck with me. She said, "Always expect the best but prepare for the worst." She expressed to me that I've always had her and if he decided to be present in my life or not, she would always be there for me. My dad had made my day better. I knew that he'd be there for me.

Chapter Two

DIFFERENT ADDRESSES, DIFFERENT ACCESSES

My mom and I moved with my big brother and his fiancé until our house was ready. It was cool living there, a different environment. I didn't switch schools, but my younger brother did. My mom dropped me off at school every morning, and I would just catch the school bus to my grandmother's house, where she would pick me up after school. My big sister had run away from the group home, so I got to see her for a while.

One Friday after school, my mom came to pick me up from my grandma's, and we were supposed to stop by to see my little brother at his dad's house. We pulled up to the house, and there was a familiar woman standing on the porch with my brother's dad. My mom didn't even park the car well when she hopped out, and she and the woman started fighting. The car was still rolling, so I turned it off and jumped out to help my mom. My sister was already out of the car and was being held by my brother's dad. My brother's dad grabbed my sister and me in his arms and squeezed us together. I couldn't believe what was happening because my brother's dad was the only stepdad we knew. He lived with us for most of our childhood. I resented him growing up because he was a real loudmouth and the disciplinarian of our household. Yet, I never thought I would see the day he would be with another woman. The woman pressed charges on my mom, causing her to be incarcerated and me having to move with my grandma. Although I always had a good time at my grandmother's house, I was reluctant to live with her.

At first, I felt like I had to be guarded without my mom. I was made aware of the difference between my siblings and me. The difference was that they had options when things happened with them, and I was always feeling forced to adjust to new environments. Usually, when something occurred, I would be sent to my God sister's house. My God mom had passed when I was much younger, but my God sisters still embraced me. I had no doubt that they genuinely loved me, and they were literally heaven-sent. My God-grandmother was a Jehovah's Witness, so I would attend the Kingdom Hall and field service on Saturdays. I, too, knocked on doors and asked, "Are you ready for the return of Jehovah?" I enjoyed reading the Watchtower too. I felt stable when I was with my God family. I never felt too needy or out of place. I wasn't raised in the church. My mom read the Bible, quoted scripture, and played gospel on Sundays, but we only went to church on occasions. I attended church with one of my mom's close friends sometimes, too, until she stopped coming around.

Living with my grandmother was better than I thought. She cooked, and not just basic food. She cooked soul food; She cooked greens, okra, and black-eyed peas, cornbread, and neck bones. She cooked me breakfast on the weekends. She made the best Kool-Aid. Originally, I was concerned about my privacy because most times, when I saw my grandmother, we were having a gathering. I was able to get to know my grandmother better when I lived with her. I grew a special love for her. I would go play her numbers for her and she made sure I had some change left over. My uncle lived with her as well. So, I would get money from him, and I would sit on his waterbed until he got rid of it. On the weekends, my grandmother went out of town to gamble, so I either stayed with my aunt or she'd ask me if I had a friend's house I could stay over. She always put money aside, and she advised me never to go anywhere broke. She also advised me to never spend my last dime.

Chapter Two—DIFFERENT ADDRESSES, DIFFERENT ACCESSES

She made sure I kept my hair done at my mom's request, and she would clean my room after me even when I thought it was already clean. I saw a lot of my mom in my grandmother. How she cleaned and how she liked things. We were eating at the table one morning and my grandma and I shed tears together over a conversation about my mom. She wanted my mom to leave my brother's dad. I bonded with her, and I needed to release some of the despair that I pretended wasn't there. I observed how she smashed her greens and cornbread together and ate with her hands.

I had gotten into trouble at school. I begged my teacher not to call my grandma, but she threatened to send me to the principal if I didn't give her the number. She called my grandma, and my grandma flipped the script. I was shaking because I was certain that my grandma would chastise me. "Don't call me. She is going through something. Leave her alone, dammit," my grandma berated. I felt bad for my science teacher because no one listened to her in that class. I was not even among the worst of her students. I felt that she was just taking her frustration out on me because I was an easy target. I had just gotten out of my seat without permission when only three people were sitting in the whole class. My mom stayed in jail for two months, and I was relieved that she was home. My grandmother was amazing, but I missed my mom.

Bowen Homes was different. A shootout could be happening in the building next to you in broad daylight and you'd see people casually walking like the bullets had their name on the *do not hit list*. I once witnessed a drive-by shooting and robbery in broad daylight. I was on my way to the store to buy my grandma some skins when a drive-by robbery took place right at the street I was approaching. I was so startled that I couldn't scream. It happened so quickly that I froze in shock. Some dudes on the patio laughed at me and asked me if I was scared, as if it wasn't a normal reaction to something like that. They offered me to stand on the porch with them, and I did. I was afraid to walk to the store, but I still went. It wasn't all bad, though. Some of the best days of my life were in Bowen Homes. Walking home after-school with my friends, jumping the fence in the field to take the shortcut, the library, the corner stores, the food spots, getting wet with the fire hydrant, and watching my uncles play golf in my grandmother's backyard. My uncles dressed in their finest to play golf in the hood. There was a school right in the middle of the hood. I didn't attend that school, but my mom did and most of the kids in the neighborhood did too. Everyone was family; that was the best part.

After moving from Bowen Homes, we never lived in another apartment. We moved to a community that had hills like San Francisco. I was so happy when I first arrived at the little yellow house with a backyard full of kudzu. Originally, it was just my mom and I living together. She worked at the Ritz Carlton, so I would be home by myself when she wasn't there. My mom would leave me money under her mattress and write letters with directions on them on how to manage my day. I later found out that my friend, Twin, lived up the street, so I would hang out with her and her twin brother. My mom advised me to learn to catch the Marta bus so I could go downtown sometimes, and that is exactly what I did. She educated me on some of the familiar routes and instructed me to ask questions when I was uncertain. She said to use my judgment and don't be naïve when asking strangers for directions. Things were simple. My mom seemed happy, and I had the freedom to do what I wanted.

December 8, 2007, my mom hosted a watch party for the Mayweather Vs. Ricky Hatton fight. That was the first time that my family gathered at my mom's new place. My mom was preparing food, and I was helping to organize when it dawned on me that it was my dad's birthday. I asked him about his birthday the day that I met him. By the time I realized that it was his birthday, it was already dawn. I called him and told him, Happy birthday. He shared that he was full and that he was relaxing. Then, I challenged him. "You forgot to tell me Happy birthday," I said. He apologized to me and told me that if I reminded him, he would never forget it again. "It was December 2nd," I shared. "Oh, Happy birthday to you," he responded.

At that moment, it was instilled in my mind that my dad was not sincere about establishing a relationship with me. I asked him where he lived, and he said, Douglasville, Georgia. "Oh, that is not too far," I declared. I heard a woman in the background, and he stated that she was my sister. When he said I had a sister, it triggered me because of several reasons. My father met me when I was three and never initiated a relationship with me, that was his second time coming into my life, and his conversation wasn't appealing as if he wanted to get to know me. Aside from that, he had other children that he also neglected. I stuttered a little and restated, "my sister." He responded, "Yes, with my wife." "You have a wife?" I asked. "Yes, I have been married for ten years; your mom knows that," he replied. He then asked me about my mom and started telling me things about her from the past. The conversation shifted from being about him and me and more about my mom. He seemed more interested in the topic of my mom. "Yeah, your mama was something else. Man, she…" "I have to go help with something. Call me back whenever you can," I interjected. My mom didn't really call me. My feelings were hurt. I put on some miss-match socks and walked around the house to find my mom. She wasn't inside. My aunt was sitting on the porch and let me know that my mom had left with my uncle to the liquor store. I went to my room, changed my clothes, and headed out to chill with Derrick. Derrick was my neighbor and my crush. I met

Derrick when my little brother moved back with us. My little brother brought Derrick to our house along with his nephew and a classmate that I had known for years. Derrick's nephew and my little brother were around the same age, and Derrick was just a year older than me. We blushed as soon as we saw one another. I never really cared about boys before I met him, but he had me at hello. When my mom saw them on the porch, she invited them inside because she needed help moving around furniture. She wasted no time asking which one of them liked me. My classmate pointed to Derrick. They didn't know that it was a setup question. He wasn't my boyfriend because I wasn't allowed to date. The time we spent together wasn't personal at first. My mom was strict with me about boys because my big sister was already a pregnant teen. She had zero tolerance. Her philosophy: "Don't nothing come from a dick but a baby or a disease." My little brother begged me not to talk to Derrick too. He said that all they do is talk about "bussin" girls, and he didn't want me to be just another girl to him. Although my little brother was five years younger than me, he was overprotective of me. The following week, I told Queen about Derrick. Queen already knew of him. She described him to make sure we were talking about the same person. "He tall, dark skin, with twists in his hair?" she inquired. "Yep," I smiled. Queen got up from her seat and came back with one of our classmate's binders. It had the girl's name and Derrick's name with a big heart in the middle displayed on a sheet of notebook paper. I didn't even press the issue because Derrick wasn't my boyfriend and Queen kept silent about it too.

When I wanted Derrick to notice me, I would walk to the end of the street and check the mailbox or throw something in the trash. The trash can was on the side of the house, so he would make a noise that attracted my attention to him. That wasn't something that we practiced together; it was just something that we did. I knew I couldn't show any signs that I wanted him around my mom. He, on the other hand, pretended that he didn't really like me but always wanted me around him. The street was too quiet for Derrick's family to be home. His mom would be sitting on the porch playing music most days, or he and his nephew would be on their motorcycles. His grandmother lived in a house on an adjoining street, so I headed that way. When I reached the front of the house, Derrick's grandmother was outside and called Derrick to the front for me. That was a first for me. I never was bold enough to be at his grandmother's house without my little brother. He came out to the street and immediately started wrestling with me. His little hits hurt, and he was fast. I would be out of breath trying to beat him up. Our relationship wasn't sentimental. I never spoke about anything personal to Derrick. He just had a way of naturally making me feel at ease. I sat on the porch watching him play with his nieces until they had to go into the house. We were basically hugged up until it was time to go into the house. Then, we walked back on our street and parted ways.

I walked into the house, and my mom started yelling at me, asking about my whereabouts. "Where you been? It's 9:00," she investigated. "We were worried about your ass," she added. I explained, "I was with Derrick right up the str-" She slapped me so hard that my ears immediately started ringing. Tears started falling down my face and I faintly heard my aunt say, "You didn't have to slap her like that; she said she was right up the street." My mom and aunt went back and forth as I stood before everyone with my hand over my face. "Say you sorry," my mom demanded. "I'm sorry for staying out so late," I replied as I walked to my room.

Christmas had come and gone, and I didn't receive a computer, much less a call from my dad. I was disappointed, but I couldn't cry about it at first because I had a good Christmas. My older brother, my brother's dad, and my mom provided my Christmas.

It wasn't like I had anything to miss about my dad. After Winter break, I asked my brother what our dad got him for Christmas. At first, he lied and said that our dad had bought him a game system and some shoes. When I told him that he promised me a computer but didn't keep his word, he said, "Man, that nigga ain't get me shit." I comforted him and told him that we didn't need him. Then we walked in our two separate crowds of friends. It was inevitable that we would become cool. Most of the time, when I would visit Bowen Homes, he'd see me and ask for a dollar. I would always see one of my uncles at my grandmother's house and ask for money or sit in their face long enough for them to offer. He would see me coming from the candy lady sometimes and try to fight me for my money. We'd be wrestling and laughing until I finally gave him a dollar. Bowen Homes was torn down and everybody spread out. My school was torn down too. The school system was changing and rezoning.

The school ended up being relocated within walking distance from my house. I met a girl named Tosha and her family on the way to school one morning. They were from Tallahassee, Florida, and had just moved into the neighborhood. Several Apartment complexes were over the hill from my community. They were all within walking distance, and many of my peers lived nearby. I had a friend, who I had known since Elementary School, that lived in one of the communities. Tia and I didn't hang out much in elementary, but we did when my school relocated. I visited Tia often because her mom was cool. Her mom was more lenient than my mom. Tia's apartments were much like Bowen Homes. They were brick and dangerous. I wasn't the type to be too much involved in other people's hood, so I stayed inside when I visited. Tia lived in the front, right at the entrance, so it was convenient for me to walk to her house and back without walking all around the hood. Tia and I didn't have much in common, especially not academically. Tia was spoiled and disrespected her mom anytime she was told no. She was boy crazy too. I loved to be around her because she was funny. I loved her because it was never a dull moment around her, and she did what she wanted. Her mom was the candy lady in their apartments, so Tia stayed supplying the snacks. We would go to Six Flags White Water on a budget and have the time of our life. When I was bored, all I had to do was call Tia.

Chapter Three

BOOKS BEFORE BOYS BECAUSE BOYS MAKE BABIES

When school was in session, I was serious about my academics. I earned honor roll every year, and I was known for being smart. I never made all A's though. Math was my weakness. I would excel in subjects such as reading, writing, and language arts. I was a part of the All-star after-school program and won a writing contest that qualified my school to enter for the district. I had to write another essay on the topic: "Why are After-school Programs important." I was given the option to submit the same essay or write another one. I chose to keep the same one. When we were in the venue, I had a feeling that my essay wasn't going to win. I didn't do my best work, and I underestimated my opponents. My essay won second place against all the schools in the district. A Mayes High school student won 1st place. Mayes High school was my high school's rival school. We had always lost to them in sports, and what were the odds of the two schools winning 1st and 2nd in yet another competition. The price was only a $25 gift card for second place, but my mom was still so proud of me. My teacher came over and spoke great things about me, and my mom was smiling from ear to ear.

My mom allowed me to dye my hair honey blonde in the 7th grade and the color became a part of my identity. I wore my hair short like a grown woman and I learned to style it myself. I started wearing wedges too. You couldn't tell me anything. Once I got to school late because I had overslept, and the secretary asked me if I had an older boyfriend. The other administrator looked at her confused, and she said, "She always have her hair cut, her eyebrows waxed, and sometimes she wears heels." I expressed thanks to her and told her that I wasn't dating. Little did she know, my mom cut and colored my hair at home and shaped me up in the back with a razor. I used a razor to experiment on my eyebrows. "My mom just allows me to express myself," I responded. That was the truth. My mom had always experimented with her hair, and I was curious. That was my favorite thing about my mom. She was versatile. She always expressed the importance of good hygiene and confidence. When I would get my hair done, she would say, "They gone try to fight you now." We played dress-up a lot in my Elementary school days. My friends loved to come over to my house. My mom was a fashionista. She had plenty of clothes, hats, and heels that we would try on and model. Everywhere I went, people would say I looked just like my mom.

My sister ran away all the time and this time, she had run away and came back pregnant. We knew who her baby dad was and that he had frequent run-ins with the law. My mom hated the thought of her being around me pregnant, but she was so happy about the baby. It was revealed that my sister was having a baby girl, and our family hosted her a beautiful baby shower at my grandma's house. My mom was dating this guy and she would spend the night with him frequently. Although my sister was the oldest, my mom would leave me in charge because she didn't trust her to do the right things. She told me to keep the house phone with me and don't let my sister use it. I didn't keep the phone with me, but I was monitoring it. I was in my room journaling when the phone rang. I got up and got the phone and went to my room. My sister bombarded the door that I had almost shut. I put my body against the door to keep her out. "Who Is that?" she asked. "None of your business, mama said you can't use the phone," I asserted. She burst

Chapter Three—BOOKS BEFORE BOYS BECAUSE BOYS MAKE BABIES

the door open, and I fell on the floor. She answered and it was her baby daddy. I started reaching for the phone, and we ended up fighting. My sister didn't punch me, but I was punching her. She threw me on the ground and put her feet on my stomach. I couldn't breathe. She didn't let me up until I was stiff. I got up and caught my breath. I started screaming, running through the house. "Yeah, I beat your head hurt!" I yelled. "I hate you," I added. "You only can use your weight because I was beating that head in," I continued to yell through the house. "I didn't punch you because I know I will hurt you," my sister claimed. "I let you get them licks because I know ma would be mad if I beat you up," she yelled. I was so mad I ran into her room, which was a small bedroom the size of an average walk-in closet and grabbed some pills that I saw. I poured the iron pills into the air conditioner vent and down the toilet. I went into the room and shut the door before I heard, "My iron pills!" in a distressed tone. The next thing I knew, my sister was busting in my room, tossing my things around. She flipped my mattress. Then, she grabbed my journal and started tearing up the pages. My eyes filled with tears. My sister started preaching to me about how I took it too far. We were going back and forth the whole evening. I didn't tell my mom because I didn't want her to get in trouble. My mom was excessive when she would get upset. She called us bitches and hoes, and if we talked back, she would kick us out of the house. Well, I would get sent away. My sister didn't talk back. I did, though. My mom couldn't stand that. She would say, "Shyla might do what she does, but she doesn't talk back; that red bitch always has to have the last word." I hated when she would tell me to go find my daddy when she'd go on her rants. My mom would be really close to whoever didn't make her mad at the time. That caused a division between my siblings and me. One would not communicate with the other to stay in my mom's good graces. I would never say anything disrespectful out loud. Most of the time,

I would mumble under my breath. I would get sent to my God sister's house. My godsister never hesitated to get me.

My English teacher Ms. Steele was my favorite class because she was really relaxed. She would chastise anyone who tried to act up in her class, but she was relaxed most of the time. She wore big hair and had an accent. I think she was from Sierra Leone. She talked fast when someone would get on her nerves. All my teachers were amazing, though. One day, I was sitting in my seat with my legs crossed in what we called "Indian style" next to my classmate Hydro. Hydro, short for Alejandro, was African American despite his name. He was maybe 5'6, had pretty light brown eyes, and was soft-spoken. Hydro and I were cool only by our association of mutual friends. Hydro was sitting slouched in his seat, twisting his hair when I turned to adjust how I was sitting. "Damn that thang phat girl," he blurted to me unexpectedly. I didn't expect to feel so humiliated, but I did. "I'm about to tell on you," I warned. "Man tell on me for what shawty?" He responded. I turned back and finished my last few questions on my assignment. When I went to turn it in, I whispered to my teacher what Hydro said to me. Ms. Steele ordered Hydro to get out of her classroom. She went on to tell him how he hadn't completed any assignments, but he had so much to say. I turned and walked back towards my seat, and Hydro argued, "Aww, you snitched; you lame as hell." "That wasn't even anything bad; it was a compliment, really." I waved bye to Hydro and walked over to the table where Tia was sitting. Tia and our classmate were joking back and forth. Tia was known to be a comedian. She loved to joke, so I don't even know why that girl thought she had more jokes than her. Tia had messed up teeth, so the girl made a joke about her teeth. Everyone knew Erica had bad breath, but we just never said it out loud. Tia started talking about her breath, and the girl got mad and started threatening to beat her up. Tia was pregnant, so I stood up to make it known that I would defend her. Our other classmate stood up too and said, "You definitely will get beat up about my friend." Ms. Steele told us to get out and go to the assistant principal's office. The principal's office was just a few doors down from our classroom. Ms. Steele stepped out and deemed me the ringleader of the commotion. Ms. Motley, our assistant principal, was a sweetheart. She didn't suspend me. She just asked what happened and told me that as a friend, I should encourage my friends to do the right thing so that they won't need defending. I smiled. Ms. Motley complimented my smile. I dismissed her compliment and brought to the light that my teeth were crooked. "Thank you, was going to their designated teachers to get their scores that entailed if we spent our summer in summer school or not. I walked into my Homeroom class, and most students were excited. When I approached the front of the line, my teacher made a sad face. I stomped my feet and started swaying side to side. She said, "It's ok, you only failed math, and you will go to Summer school and pass." I still felt bad because I wasn't used to failing. I became distracted by her shirt. She had on a green shirt with pink letters that read, "AKA." I read it as it sounded, and she corrected me and said it was an acronym for her sorority. Then, it started making sense as to why all her things were pink and green. She said that I could become one too if I chose to attend College.

That day after school, I walked to Tia's house. She told me that she wasn't coming back to school. She said something about her mom having a meeting and she would have to go to another school. I couldn't even say anything because what could I say? Tia really didn't like school in the first place. I stayed for a while then walked back home.

My sister was on the porch when I reached my house. We were conversing when she but I hate smiling because my teeth are messed up," I responded. "I said your smile is pretty. You don't have to have perfect teeth to have a pretty smile," Ms. Motley corrected. Ms. Motley sent me back to the classroom with instructions to apologize to Ms. Steele and my classmates.

At the end of the school day, the standardized test results were back, and everyone stepped from the porch and said, "Who is that with that red scarf on holding hands with Derrick?" "It's probably his sister," I said with certainty. I know my sister had 20/20 vision, unlike me, but Derrick had three sisters, so I just assumed it was one of them. My sister replied, "That is not his sister; come look." My heart dropped to my stomach because it wasn't his sister. It was Shelly. She went to my school, and she was Tia's other best friend. I couldn't bear to watch her and Derrick holding hands walking up the hill, so I told my sister to pretend we didn't notice them. Derrick really brought that girl around and had the audacity to be holding hands with her. We weren't official, but I thought we had something special. I called Tia and asked her if she knew about Shelly and Derrick. She told me that Shelly had mentioned him, and she let her know that he and I were seeing each other. I shared with Tia that I witnessed Derrick and Shelly walking up the hill holding hands. Tia said, "Girl, she was desperate to come up there and she knew he talked to you, but that is on her." I told Tia I would call her back later. My feelings were so hurt. My little brother was over at Derrick's house with his nephew. When the sun went down, I went on the porch and my little brother, Derrick's nephew, and Derrick came from across the street. I didn't say anything. I pretended to be unconcerned. Derrick came and started hitting me like he didn't spend the whole day with another girl. I pushed him away and gave him the silent treatment. He continued to wrestle me, and then I asked, "Didn't you just leave your girl?" Derrick denied that she was his girlfriend and claimed that she was just his homie. I relaxed and allowed him to embrace me before brushing him off. I called Tia back. As soon as she answered, I said, "Girl, why Derrick came back over here like nothing happened. Tia replied, "Girl, because he like you and Shelly so stupid cause y'all live right across the street, he ain't going to leave you alone." I persuaded Tia to call Shelly on the three-way while my line was muted. "Ok, what do you want me to say?" she asked. "Just have a regular conversation and ask her where she been, but don't make it obvious," I instructed. Tia called Shelly and Shelly was hesitant to tell her business at first. She had just got out of the shower. I cringed, hearing her voice. Besides her going to my school, I knew nothing about Shelly. I wanted to know everything about her after seeing her with Derrick.

It was a week before the 8th grade dance, and I was waiting by my big brother's car so we could go dress shopping. At first, I was told that I wasn't going to attend. I eavesdropped on a conversation between my mom and older brother and heard my mom say, "She is going to the dance. She ain't got to miss her dance because of her." I didn't know what was going on. My brother and I went out to find dresses. We chose a midi, gold dress with a matching scarf. My mom already knew who she wanted to do my hair. She had a friend who owned a shop. My hair was styled in a blonde pixie with spikes. I felt so good, like no one was doing it like me. On the day of the dance, my sister-in-law pulled up in her yellow mustang to drop me off. We pulled up playing "Put On" by Kanye West and Jeezy, but no one was outside, so we turned around and went back to the house. We waited a while and my big brother took me back to his old skool. Everyone was pulling up. I walked into the building, and one of my peers had on the same dress but longer. I searched around for my friends, and I heard that they had been suspended for fighting. Allegedly, they jumped a girl. I just started mingling and dancing with whoever was there.

Summer school ended up being fun. We had three teachers in each class to review certain subjects. We weren't in school for 8 hours like typical school days. I became cool with a girl named Angel. I started going over to her house after summer school. She lived with her aunt, and they were the candy lady. I came to know that she smoked weed and I started smoking with her. Sometimes it made me laugh, and other times it made me sleepy. Angel and I would smoke, eat snacks, and be on the computer all day. We took turns updating our Myspace profiles. Our friend CeCe stayed down the street, and sometimes she would come over, or we would go over to her house. Angel was not the type to sit still. She loved to be out and about. She and her big sister were well known. We always had free entry to clubs because Angel's older brother was a club promoter. We would get dressed and do our makeup. Angel and her sister both did hair, so I would pay either of them to do my hair. Sometimes, they did it for free. Most times, Angel would do my hair for free if she had some marijuana, but she would take all day. She would never finish because we would always have somewhere to go. I liked to get my hair done in one sitting but messing around with Angel, I'd be walking around with incomplete braids for days.

I was walking outside to catch the bus when my neighbor's dog ran out and started barking at me. The dog was little, but I was terrified. I started throwing sticks at it and it just dodged them and kept barking. I didn't throw the sticks to hit the dog. I just hoped maybe it would be more interested in the sticks and run away. I screamed and threw things at that dog until I heard the school bus coming. I had to make a run for the bus because attendance had to be 100% to pass summer school. Getting held back was not an option. I ran towards the bus and my flats flipped off my feet. The dog ran up closer to me. Then, the owner's granddaughter came outside and directed the dog back to the porch. By that time, the bus had stopped and opened the door. I ran and grabbed my shoe. I guess the bus driver found that amusing because she was laughing, and she hadn't even seen the whole thing.

Once summer school was over, I went over to my God sister's house for the weekend. I called my mom and my sister answered. "Mama got locked up," she said in a nonchalant way. My stomach immediately dropped to my feet even though I was at my God cousin's party having a great time just a second before. "Why, what happened?" I asked. "Girl, I don't know they said she had a warrant," she replied. I didn't even tell my godsister. I just walked around pretending like everything was ok.

Chapter Four
NEW ADDITION

My mom had a family friend come stay with my sister and me. She needed somewhere to live, and we needed an adult in the house. My little brother went to live with his father. Everything was fine until my sister came to me crying. My sister rarely cried. I confronted my mom's friend. I told her that we didn't need her to keep us. We could take care of ourselves if she was going to disrespect my sister. She argued with me like I was a grown woman. She was trying to prove herself in front of her boyfriend. He had just been released from jail. His presence disturbed me. She called my aunt on us to form an alliance with them. She made it seem as though we were disrespecting her, and my aunt came to her defense, calling us grown and claiming that we needed her. Little did she know my sister and I had been keeping ourselves for years. We didn't need her or her extra guest.

My mom called and confirmed what I already knew. Her friend was shady. My mom had no clue that anyone else was living at the house with us. She asked did I get my hair done, and when I revealed to her that I didn't, she immediately became upset and instructed me to tell her former friend to leave. She had purchased her man fresh air-force ones and Nike sweatsuits with my money.

When I hung up with my mom, I called Angel. She asked me to come spend the night over at her house. Angel and I went over to her brother's baby mom's house so that she could spend time with her niece. We took pictures by her brother's Camaro and uploaded them to Facebook. Her brother's ex complimented my walk and told me that she wished she walked with her back straight like me. I didn't even know that was a thing, but since she was a grown woman telling me that, I figured it was important. When we got back to Angel's place, we packed and caught the bus to my house. When we arrived at my house, it was late. My sister was there alone, we thought. Angel found a blunt in my mom's bathroom, and we smoked it without thinking twice. We fixed some noodles and snuggled in my mom's king-size bed that she liked high from the floor. We watched a lifetime movie until I fell asleep. I was rudely awakened by Angel rocking me side to side, "Adore, that boy is crawling on the floor." "Huh," I said, still half asleep. "That boy, your sister's boyfriend down there," she reiterated. I jumped up and tossed myself to the end of the bed. My sister's baby dad was literally crawling on the floor. He was looking for his weed that we had smoked. "Where is my weed at?" He asked. "I don't know about no weed. Get off the floor; you're scaring my friend," I demanded. "Y'all smoked my weed," He responded. "No, we didn't get out of here," I demanded. He stood up, walked into the other room, and told my sister that we smoked his weed. My mom would've been upset if she knew that my sister's baby father was staying over, especially while she wasn't there. That's the kind of behavior that she expected from my sister. I wouldn't dare tell on her, though. Besides, I was not perfect either. The next morning, we had more marijuana but nothing to roll it with, so we rolled it up with notebook paper and attempted to smoke it. Our throats were burning so bad. My sister called us some young junkies, and we laughed. I was spending way too much time with Derrick. He came over to see my niece and we always ended up messing around. We didn't have sex at first. He did finger me, though, and my sister walked right in and caught us. As soon as she turned the corner, he slipped his hands from in my panties. "Oh my God, y'all nasty. I saw you with your hands in her panties, and her eyes fire red," she

Chapter Four—NEW ADDITION

said. "No, he wasn't," I lied. Fingering me made Derrick curious. He said, "That thang was wet." I can admit that it made me curious too. I always liked feeling him close. That is why I loved to wrestle with him because we always ended up tangled. He always smelled good and never smelled like outside like my little brother did. I overcame my fear of motorcycles because of him. He demanded that I ride with him, assuring me that "he got me." One time Derrick and his nephew were riding their bikes and my brother was on the back with Derrick. Derrick's girlfriend was on the opposite side of the street in front of Derrick's house, watching as well. I came out to the end of the street to talk to Empress. Empress was a girl who I had met in Bowen Homes. Empress was light-skinned with big eyes, and long pretty hair. She was slim with a booty that sat on her back, which made it appear bigger when she wore certain clothes. I clicked with her immediately, but we didn't talk much. She was always with her siblings or her family. When Derrick's nephew asked if one of us wanted to ride with him. Empress declined, but I rode on the back with him. When we got around the block, they both stopped their bikes. I couldn't hear exactly what they were saying to one another. I just know that Derrick's nephew signaled me to get on the bike with Derrick. My little brother didn't want to change places with me, but Derrick convinced him. I was smiling from ear to ear because it felt good that Derrick was pursuing me and not the other way around. I had a huge crush on Derrick, and everyone knew it even though I tried hard to mask it. I didn't want to be extra around Derrick; I used my absence instead. Derrick was the first guy I was sexually attracted to, and I didn't know if it was safe to tell him. It hurt me that he had a girlfriend, but I knew that I couldn't openly date him, so I didn't make a big deal out of it.

When I returned home for the night, Tia called me. She ambushed me with Shelly on the three-way. I wasn't surprised. Tia always presented herself as if she had favoritism for me over Shelly, but I knew that Tia and Shelly had more things in common than Tia and me. They spent more time together too. Tia told me Shelly's business, so I knew that she told my business to her too. The difference between Shelly and me was that I told Tia everything. Tia said that Shelly didn't tell much of her business. She would always say, "You just have to be around her to know her." I felt like Shelly was just smart and knew not to share too much. "I just want to know are you talking to my man," Shelly blurted. "Don't worry about me," I argued. "You knew we talked before you started going with him," I added. "Girl, he doesn't even claim you. You are his neighbor," Shelly contended. "Well, keep thinking that then," I responded. "He is my boyfriend, and you know that," she said. Then she hung up the phone. I asked Tia why she called me with her on the phone, and Tia claimed that Shelly kept asking her. Tia had confirmed everything that I already knew.

I told Queen about what happened between Shelly and me. Queen saw her in the school restroom and bumped her. Later Shelly told Tia that she wasn't scared of us because she had "goons" too. We weren't even studying Shelly for real. After school, I stayed at Twin's house. Our other schoolmate, T, had gotten off the bus with her, so she was at their house, visiting too. It was a sunny day with just enough breeze. We waited as Twin settled and fixed her snack. I notified them that I needed to go home to let my sister know where I was, and I'd be back. Twin and T came with me since neither of them had been to my house before. The street was quiet and empty. We went inside and talked to my sister for a moment. T and Twin both were mesmerized by my sister's pregnant belly. I grabbed a snack, and we all headed back down the road and over the hill to Twin's house. When we reached the bottom of the hill, Derrick's dog came running towards us. We all screamed and scattered like roaches. T and I ran up towards my house and jumped

Chapter Four—NEW ADDITION

on top of Derrick's mom's car. Derrick ran past us and secured the dog making direct eye contact with me. I could tell he was forced to be a part of it. "Get off my car y'all." "Please get out of my car," Derrick's mom pleaded. "Get your dog then," T proposed. Standing on the side observing was Shelly, Empress and two of Derrick's older sisters. Shelly set me up. I never jumped anyone, except the lady who touched my mom. My sister came outside and stood on the porch. "If that dog had bit my sister, I would've beat y'all ass one by one," she yelled from the porch. We hopped off her car and went on the porch with my sister. I had to tell Twin and T what transpired between Shelly and me because they had no idea what was going on. I hated that they had to be involved. They stayed and hung out with me until Twin and I walked T to the Marta bus stop. Twin watched me walk back to the house, then headed home.

Later that night, my phone rang with an unknown number. I answered the phone, and it was one of Derrick's sisters. She had me on the speakerphone. "All I got to say is if anything happens to my brother, y'all going to have a big problem," said Derrick's sister. I didn't know what Shelly had told them, but I cared about Derrick and had no reason to harm him. I wasn't about to let his sister just threaten me, though. "Girl, please! If I wanted something to happen, it would've happened," I said in a calm tone. "I don't have any issues with Derrick or none of you," I said officially. She hung up and texts started coming in instantaneously. Shelly was calling us broke, saying that we were on section 8 and that we were from the hood. I knew that Derrick's mom's inquiring mind had to be supplying Shelly with the information because it was random and off-topic. A little altercation between Shelly and me transpired into a war between two families. I called my sister in the room just so she could know what was going on in case the situation escalated beyond texting. My sister wasn't argumentative at all, but I could debate. I texted all caps, "WRONG! You can either get your facts right or spew out lies." I continued, "Do your research. This house isn't paid for with a voucher; it's paid for by hustle sweety!" "You went and told all of them lies; now it's us against y'all," I went on. "NEXT!" I sent it in all caps. No Response. That was about five texts back-to-back. I really didn't want to mess up my relationship with Derrick by exposing his family's business. I thought that Empress had crossed me too, but she came to me and confirmed what I already knew. Shelly told them a bunch of lies. I saw Derrick's sisters and mom a few times and they didn't say anything to me. I was glad. I desperately wanted everything to just roll over before my mom came home. Derrick lasted two days without coming over to my house, and he was back again.

My mom had an attitude when she came home. She criticized how we took care of the house. I prayed when I heard she was getting out of jail. I prayed that she would be in a good mood. The transition was just weird; it was back to business as usual. She called around handling matters concerning bills and whatever else. My mom had a hard exterior. I often wondered what went on in her thoughts and how she kept going. I felt empathy for her no matter what. She was all I had. My sister's due date was supposed to be on my birth date, but it didn't happen. I was getting dressed for school when she was having contractions. I was so excited. I had been talking about my niece's arrival ever since I found out the gender. I was super excited that she would be a Sagittarius just like me. My sister allowed us to name her. My mom suggested that she name her "Gloria." My sister and I burst out laughing. "No, mama, that's too old skool," said my sister, still laughing. My sister proclaimed that she had chosen a name, but we could still choose another name that would possibly be her middle or first name. "I like the name Patience," I intervened. "Patient, like in the hospital?" my mom asked. "No Patience, like to have patience," I responded. My sister agreed that it was a pretty name. The name was inspired by the movie *Cat Woman*, starring Halle Berry.

When I came home from school, my mom shared with me that my sister had given birth to my niece and that she would come home soon. I couldn't wait. When I came home the next day, there was my niece in her car seat on top of my bed. She was so beautiful that it was breathtaking. My mom suggested her nickname be China because of her eyes. It was love at first sight for me. I thought that she was my baby. I would go into my sister's room to get her when my sister would be resting. Sometimes she would be crying at 2 am on a school night, and I didn't care. I would change her, fix her a bottle, and cuddle her. She was the sweetest baby ever. She didn't cry much unless she was hungry. She played well by herself, and she was affectionate. She had such cute lips and curly hair. She was a chocolate drop. My sister booked her a photoshoot, and I carried the biggest picture in front of my binder. I felt her birth was the perfect timing for my life, and I felt that she was the best thing to happen to me in my whole life. Derrick's oldest sister had a baby a few months before my sister had Patience, and gossip about whose baby looked the best was buzzing on our street. Both babies were pretty. Derrick would come over and play with Patience. He was the person who influenced me to call her chocolate drop.

I was coming from Twin's house when I saw Empress and her sisters in the middle of the street. I thought that it was unusual because Empress never brought anyone with her before when she came to visit Derrick's nephew. I went into the house before I came back outside to see what she was up to. My mom was already observing whatever was happening through the glass storm door. "Her hot ass out there keeping up shit," my mom judged. I was eager to know what was happening, so I asked my mom if she needed me to do anything before I went outside. "You have homework?" She asked. "Nope," I answered. I went outside and stood by my mailbox and asked Empress what was going on. Empress went on to say that she and Shelly were in a verbal altercation the night before. "I just wanted to see if that bitch was really about that life," Empress explained as I stepped away. My mom was coming outside and overheard Empress use profanity. "Why are you out here keeping up drama girl, I didn't know you were like that," my mom addressed. Empress apologized to my mom and stated that Shelly had too much mouth. My mom changed her disposition from authoritative to calmer. Shelly never came outside. Empress walked up the hill to Derrick's grandma's house. A few moments later, out came Derrick's mom approaching our porch. I had already given my mom the 411 on what transpired when she first got out. I completely downplayed any feelings for Derrick in the process. My mom invited her inside. "This has to stop," Derrick's mom commanded. "Yeah, I told Adore don't be out there keeping up no shit and to stay away from that hot ass lil girl," she lied. Derrick's mom revealed that she had a conversation with Derrick and his nephew as well. I found it funny how Derrick's mom tried to appear mature when she was amid the drama with Shelly and me. I found it even more hilarious that she thought that my mom was oblivious about it all. Little did she know, my mom felt compelled to invite her inside so that she could see the view. My mom took pride in her ability to decorate, and she wanted to give Derrick's mom something else to talk about. My mom confided in me that she wished she would've gone to school for interior design. I noticed that my mom had a passion for interior design and home decor because she always rearranged the house every so often, and she had no budget when purchasing home decor. I could tell that it made her happy.

Chapter Five

TRIGGER WARNING!

I became curious about sex. I knew that Derrick wanted it from me. Besides, he had already made it clear when he fingered me. My sister didn't talk to me about sex often. She did talk to me about oral sex, though. She seemed to really enjoy it. I called my friend Nya. Nya and I became close when I started. She and I had always attended the same school, but when I started talking to her best friend, she was the middle person for him to get in contact with me. Nya was reading this book called *G Spot*. The book belonged to her mother. We would spend hours on the phone and end the night with her reading me a chapter every night. That book would have me fantasizing in public about the things I would do to Derrick. The sex scenes were so vivid.

The next day at school, Queen got into a fight in our math class. The whole fight seemed to appear in slow motion, but Queen won. Queen sat next to me in that class, and when my teacher came over to confront the two girls, she glimpsed at my niece's picture in the front of my binder. She and I engaged in conversation, and she disclosed that she had one daughter, but she wished she would've had more kids. She showed me pictures of her daughter. I told her that my sister could use some support, and she maybe could use a Godmother for my niece. I told her I would have a word with my sister. I also told her that we lived within walking distance from the school. Her eyes lit up like a Christmas tree. I spoke with my sister that evening, and she said that I was crazy, but she would have to feel her out before she let her baby go anywhere with her.

I wouldn't blatantly put my niece in harm's way. I had my own biases about godmothers from my experiences with my own, so a person had to be legit for me to be a reference.

My sister agreed to my niece staying over at my math teacher's house. She shed a few tears because that was her first time away from her baby. When my teacher brought my niece back, she expressed that she was exceptional. That was the first and last time that she kept her, though. My sister couldn't cope without her baby for long. Over the next few days, random people were stopping by and taking pictures of the house. Supposedly, the landlord wasn't paying the mortgage despite my mom paying rent. The house was going into foreclosure. My mom did mention that no one came to collect rent for a couple of months, but she wasn't sure what was happening. Life was lovely until the letters came in about the bank taking ownership of the house. My mom began yelling a lot more. I literally saw her tonsils once, and the veins were sharp on the side of her face. She started yelling at me, saying that I needed to get a job. "It's plenty lil girls working at Kroger and Publix," she scolded. I hated that she compared me to other people. I argued back, "You have to be 14 to work at Kroger." She told me to shut up and go find my daddy. I argued back again, "You find him." I peeped around the wall to see if she was going to come hit me. My mom called my godsister and told her to come pick me up before she hurt me because I was too grown. My sister came right away.

I started expressing how I felt in my journal. Writing was my escape. I wrote about everything until one day I came from outside to my mom waiting on me at the door. My sister had shown my mom one of my journals. "Since your life is so miserable, why don't you get the fuck out and go where it's better," my mom yelled. "You are writing all that bullshit about me in my house," She added. "I will burn that shit," she threatened. I felt so betrayed

Chapter Five—TRIGGER WARNING!

and violated. I felt like my haven was bombarded by a dark force beyond my control. I cried until I started hyperventilating. I found myself randomly crying for the next couple of days. I wouldn't cry in the open, but my heart felt heavy. I tried to cover up how I felt by being extra cheerful. The feeling wouldn't go away. I would release when I showered or when I was alone in bed at night. It seemed as if the sound of water made the tears flow from my eyes. One day, I was washing dishes, and my little brother walked into the kitchen. I quickly inhaled and wiped the tears from my face. He hopped on the counter and said, "Why are you always sad?" I looked at him, and the tears came back down. I started expressing myself to him. Even though he was five years younger than me, I felt seen by him. When I told him that I was depressed, he said, "You are strong, don't worry about Ma." Don't worry about nobody; just keep doing you like you always do." Then he wiped the tears from my face. The next day, to my surprise, my mom apologized to me. She addressed that she shouldn't have read my personal thoughts. She hugged me and left my room. I felt a sense of relief that she realized that what she did was wrong, but I still felt as though I had no safe place to express myself. I was just about to write about my sexual desires for Derrick too. Then, I really would have been in trouble.

My sister had run away again. I missed Patience. I was disappointed with my sister because she knew how much I loved my niece. She just took her away. My mom talked about her often. Most times, she sounded angry, but I knew she was hurt more than anything. She constantly talked about how she had thrown my sister that baby shower and did her best with accepting that she had a baby in the first place. She said it was like a slap her in the face for my sister to run away again. I was confused until I heard the news that my sister could be pregnant for one of her friends. The fact that her baby father was in jail assured me that if she was pregnant, the baby was by her new boyfriend. I met him before, and surprisingly, he was not a thug. He was a junior in high school, and he wore a backpack with books in it. That alone said a lot because no one wore book bags with actual books in them. People thought they were too cool to even wear a coat in the winter. My mom commented that he had to be mental to date someone who attends alternative school when he was in a regular school. I met my sister at the train station when she revealed to me that she was expecting. She told me where I could see Patience, and I promised not to tell my mom.

    My godsister called to check on me. I asked her to come get me, and she said that she would let me know later. Later that night, she called and told me to be ready. I stayed at her house for the weekend. I shared with my godsister what my sister told me. My God could keep a secret. She respected my mom, but her interest was just in me ever since her mom had passed. She brought me back home late Sunday evening, around 7:00pm. Twin, her brother, and two of their neighbors were in the middle of the street wrestling with Derrick. They were wrestling, boys against girls. As soon as I joined the game, all Derrick's hits were directed towards me. Twin's neighbor noticed and called him out. "Why are you only hitting her now," she asked irritably. "No, I'm playing with everybody, you want some of this, huh?" he said playfully, directing his attacks back at her. She laughed and started running around like everyone else. I followed the other girls. Twin said that it was time to go home, so everyone left except me, Derrick, and his nephew. Then, his nephew went into the house. Derrick and I began walking and talking. He asked where I had been all weekend, and we were having a casual conversation when I noticed he was leading me behind a duplex that had been deserted for some time. "Someone lives here now?" I asked. He started kissing me. We had never kissed with tongue before. I started pulling his shirt tight like

Chapter Five—TRIGGER WARNING!

I wanted him closer to me. He pushed me up against the brick wall and attempted to put his hands in my pants. My pants were too tight. He attempted to unbutton my pants. Then, I stopped him. "We can't do this right here, and it's late," I uttered. Derrick dropped his hand to his side and gazed at the sky before telling me to come on. He walked me home. I couldn't believe I came so close to losing my virginity.

My mom was in her bed with her knees bent, eating one of her favorite snacks and watching T.V. "You locked the door?" she asked in between her smacking on the Ruffles, cheese, and green olives. "Yes," I replied, heading towards the bathroom. The next day I was standing on the porch eating a peach when Derrick came over to bother me. "Oh, you wore a skirt today, you must want this thang for real," he teased. "Shut up, it's pretty today; nobody is studying you," I denied. It was a beautiful day. It was hot, but the sun was hidden by the trees just enough to feel the breeze on my porch. Somehow, I ended up inside Derrick's house, then his room. I was paranoid but curious. I had never been on the inside of his house. I had only imagined how it looked from my little brother's description of it. I had just given Derrick my virginity. It was nothing like everyone had described sex would be. It was painful. I almost fell behind his bed, trying to run from the pain. Derrick kept saying, "I got you. I'll go slow," but it still hurt. It was fast. We didn't kiss. He only kissed my neck. When it was over, he stayed, and I left. We did use protection, so at least I knew I wasn't pregnant. I couldn't face my mom when I got in the house. I dashed to the bathroom, and there was a little blood when I wiped. I was a little sore too. All my common sense didn't take effect when I was in the moment. I felt so played. "Why didn't I just wait?" I desperately wanted to know how Derrick felt about me. I had so many unanswered questions. Did it feel good to him? Did he still like me? Would he tell everybody? I didn't even look at him as I left his house.

Derrick came over again the next morning. He joked about telling my mom what occurred between us. I had to shut him down, quick. I explained to him why it wasn't a laughing matter at all and told him that it was bold of him to be talking about that on my porch. He should've known better because his mom was the same way about his sisters, and they were much older. "Derrick, unless you don't care about me being kicked out, homeless, and hopeless, don't tell anyone what we did," I warned. Derrick was still giggling, so I angrily turned away to walk into the house when he grabbed me from behind. "I was just playing, ok, it's between us," He assured me. Derrick and Shelly never broke up. She visited him often, and they would spend the night together at his older sister's house. My little brother was the source of all my information about Derrick. My mom would never approve of me staying over at a boy's house. I don't know what kind of parents Shelly had, but Tia told me that Shelly was rude to her mom and only respected her big sister. I felt like Derrick used me, but I still liked him. I wanted him to break up with Shelly. I couldn't even say that he treated me differently because he didn't. He used my situation to his advantage. He was curious about me, but he wanted to keep his girlfriend too. I felt so stupid and embarrassed. I didn't want to think about Derrick or be seen by him, so I started hanging out with my friend, Tosha. I walked to her house every day. Tosha lived with her aunt. She was younger than me, but she was boy crazy and dated older boys. She was able to date under the condition that she would remain transparent with her aunt about her relationships. Everything felt so nonjudgmental at their house. We would have movie night and game night every other weekend. They had a little dog that sat in the yard; I was afraid of it. Tosha would laugh at me

Chapter Five—TRIGGER WARNING!

until she turned red in the face because she would always have to hold it for me to leave the porch.

My mom came home one night and woke me up from my sleep. "Adore, have that bastard up the street ever tried you?" She asked. "Who, Ma," I asked with my eyes barely open. "That girl's uncle," she specified. I sat up in my bed. "Yes, but he never touched me," I informed my mom. I told my mom the story about Tosha's aunt's boyfriend trying to set me up. I visited Tosha one day, and he was home alone. He told me to come in, and they would be right back from the store. I called Tosha several times before coming to her house, but she didn't answer. He was on the porch when I got to her house. When she finally called me back, I was in her living room by myself. Tosha explained that her phone was dead, and she was using the car charger. She, her aunt, and little cousin were on the way to Florida, and he knew that. I didn't say a word; I just hurried out the side door while he was in the bathroom. "I knew it. I can tell he was a pervert from his eyes, my mom declared." "I didn't like his energy and I cursed his ass out in front of Larry," she added. My mom said that she threatened that if he ever tried me, she would kill him. Supposedly, he greeted my mom at the liquor store and her mother's intuition was in full force. He deserved every bit of that. Tosha later told me that her little cousin, his daughter, reported that he had touched her inappropriately in the past. He was incarcerated for domestic violence shortly after our conversation.

My little brother had already told Derrick that we were moving. Derrick came to me and asked about it, and I confirmed with him. He wasn't the type to be mushy, so he played it cool. "Bye then, Shawty," he said, seemingly nonchalant. I was sad that we were moving, but it was what it was. I was helping my mom load things in the truck when my sister appeared. My mom was already upset because she had bumped her head on a piece of furniture. She was walking out of the house, holding ice on her knot, when she caught sight of my sister. "Bye! Go back where you came from," She directed at my sister. "Who do you think you are coming back here after running away like that?" She continued. As my mom approached the end of the street, she noticed my sister's pregnant belly. "You're pregnant again!" she announced in an appalled tone. My mom continued to disparage my sister until she was out of sight. She even told my sister's new boyfriend that she was slow, and he had to be slow too to get her pregnant. The whole occurrence made me sad. I worried about my big sister. I couldn't believe she chose to get pregnant again, but I prayed for her.

When my mom suspected I was having sex. It was the usual "smelling yourself" premonition. She yelled at me about how I don't need to be fucking and that if I became pregnant, she would hate to get me an abortion, so I might as well not do it. She said, "Once you get that first piece of dick, you are not going to want to stop." Then she asked, "You fucking Adore?" In a concerned voice. "No, I'm not having sex; I don't even like boys," I lied. She confided in my big brother to give me the "talk." First, I overheard them talking. She said that I wasn't allowed to date until I was 40. My brother objected and stated that if she prohibited me from dating that I would just be sneaky or Gay. My brother held a much calmer demeanor and just told me to be honest so that I could get on birth control. Despite my mom's threatening tone, she just wanted me to do something different. I knew that beneath the tough love, she was vulnerable. I felt it was my duty to protect my mom by protecting myself.

We moved right across from what was once Bowen Homes. It appeared as empty land with wired fences that separated my history from my new reality. King Grant community was full of old brick houses that were aesthetically pleasing to my mom. She loved those old brick houses. The house was big, with three bedrooms and a huge basement. I had my own room, but the blinds crept me out, so I rarely slept in it. My mom sanitized the place as best as she could, and she put a curtain up so I wouldn't have to see the ugly blinds. She didn't like one of the bathrooms. The home was old. The appliances were outdated. The bathroom sink was held up by a stick and it was rusted. We kept that door closed. I slept with my mom most of the time and so did my little brother. The good thing was that we moved closer to Taylor. Taylor lived less than 5 minutes away in the same community. Patience's daycare was on the street right before Taylor's house, so I would visit her often and even ran into my sister sometimes. Patience's daycare was a home daycare, and the owner was a sweet older lady. She allowed me to come visit Patience at any time. She was just as in love with Patience as me and she became family, so it was inevitable that she'd be swept into the drama between my mom and sister.

My sister had to have an emergency c-section because she and her boyfriend got into a physical altercation at the train station. He pulled my sister's gold chain off her neck too. We both had just been gifted authentic necklaces. He turned out to be just like the rest of them. He even acted up in school, so he'd end up at the same alternative school as my sister. My mom was right. He wasn't the brightest star in the galaxy, after all. I joked with my sister about her turning her boyfriends crazy. There was no way a perfectly sane individual would choose to go to an alternative school when they were that close to graduating high school. It just didn't sit right with me that he was behaving like that. When I met him, he seemed like a nice guy. He was concerned about his homework and everything. He had me fooled. I asked my sister about his family and that cleared a lot of confusion for me. He didn't have a great relationship with his mom due to addiction and was raised by his grandparents. His mom was present in his adult life, but the relationship was strained. My sister was the type to hold her man down. She really loved unconditionally, and I could attest to that. All she needed was chemistry, not money, education, or anything. A sucker for love is what I called her, but all she did was laugh and deny it.

When my sister delivered my nephew, things became even more complicated for her. She had been living from place to place, which caused her to seek help from my mom. My mom agreed to let her live with us temporarily. Of course, she had a lot to say about it, but she did welcome her to the space in the basement. She complained that my nephew cried too much and too loud. The basement was carpeted and huge. There was enough space for my sister and enough space for my niece to crawl around, but there was no furniture. All my sister had was a diaper bag and some items she received from the hospital. Since my sister had a c-section, it was still hard for her to move. I walked downstairs to the basement one day to my sister crying in pain. She had urinated on herself because she couldn't move. At that moment, my heart bled for my sister. I realized how hard it was for her to manage being a single mom with two kids who were still in diapers. I also realized the shortcomings of my sister and mom's relationship. I changed my nephew's diaper and helped my sister to her feet. We struggled to the restroom, where she washed herself up. I played with my niece before I walked back upstairs to sleep with my mom. Once I laid my head on my pillow, I cried silent tears and prayed for my sister. I had never witnessed that kind of helplessness.

The next day my aunt came over to visit my mom. She went downstairs to see my sister, smiled in her face, and then gossiped about her to my mom. She talked about how my sister had nasty diapers in the basement. She could've used that same energy to help my sister, but I wasn't surprised. Our family was huge, but our immediate family was like an island of its own. My mom shared so much of our personal problems that my sister and I felt isolated. We stopped showing up to functions. Everything we did was shared with the family and my mom's friends. Sometimes she would exaggerate and add things that we didn't say or do to make herself look like a victim. She never exposed the part she played in the chaos. I hated when my mom's friends would come around because I witnessed how she portrayed us to them when she was upset, and they never checked her or said anything positive. My mom resented my sister because my sister didn't hesitate to call my grandma or my aunt when something went down. All she had to do was tell my grandma for the word to spread like wildfire. My mom still controlled the narrative because she would turn it all around and no one would care anymore. I felt suffocated because I loved my mom and my sister. I also felt lonely. I wanted to be closer to my mom, but I felt I couldn't confide in her unless it was something good. I didn't want her to feel like a failure.

Chapter Six

GRACE

I walked into the house from school playing Beyonce's "If I Were a Boy" on my small Kyocera phone. The house was quiet. I opened my mom's room door, and she was lying in bed with the TV on and curtains closed. "It smells funny in here," I uttered. "What does it smell like?" asked my mom. "Like death," I replied. The room didn't stink like a dead body. Death was just the only word I could think of to describe the smell coming from my mom's room. My mom had been eating mashed potatoes and in bed for a week. She had finally checked herself into Grady Hospital. At first, I stayed home by myself, then occasionally started staying at Taylor's and Angel's house. I found myself feeling triggered at Taylor's house, so I went over to Angel's house. Taylor and I were sitting on the bed when she and her older sister got into a verbal altercation that turned physical. It was just a regular sibling rivalry until Taylor's mom came from the other room and started attacking Taylor. I sat on the bed in shock. Taylor had a panic attack, and the ambulance was called. What she always felt had come to light. Her mom favored her sister. When Taylor expressed what she felt, her mom couldn't come up with a valid reason why she jumped in the fight instead of deescalating the situation. Taylor's house was my second home, but the dysfunction had me feeling like I was trapped in an everlasting maze searching for peace of mind.

My mom and I communicated via phone until I visited her. When she called me crying, saying that she may have Cancer. I couldn't breathe for a second. I felt like my throat closed. She disclosed that the doctor found white spots on her lungs that could have been cancerous. Nothing was set in stone, and I wanted my mom to be hopeful. She asked that I pray for her. My mom later called and updated me that she was diagnosed with Tuberculosis and not cancer. She invited my sister and me to come see her. I had no idea what Tuberculosis was, but I learned the seriousness of it when I had to wear a mask when I would visit her.

Although my sister and mom had a rough time, my sister still wanted to make my mom feel better about being hospitalized. Any form of illness in my family was frowned upon. No one openly shared their health conditions in my family, and that is why my mom discouraged visitors. When my mom was in need, she relied on us. She knew where she felt loved, but I think she gave so much of herself to people on the outside because she wanted to fill a void from her own childhood. My sister called and asked me if there was anything that I wanted to put in my mom's gift bag that she was coordinating. I just suggested fruit. My sister ended up purchasing a coloring book, the fruit, some panties, and some keepsakes. When we arrived, we learned that we had to wear masks. My mom was in good spirits. She gave me money to get my hair done. We walked next door from the hospital to buy my mom McDonald's because she said the hospital food didn't satisfy her appetite. We all shared laughs until my sister and I left. We walked to the train station, and my sister stayed with me until my train arrived. Then, we waved goodbye to one another.

When my mom came home, she moved to my grandma's house temporarily until our place was ready. My mom wasn't 100 percent recovered and she was sleeping on my grandma's couch. She had lost a lot of weight, and she was physically weak. My mom never liked to live with anyone. She prided herself on being independent, but she needed support. My mom didn't have a great experience

Chapter Six—GRACE

living with my grandma in her time of need because my grandma didn't like my mom being on the couch. My grandma was also an early bird and she frowned upon sleeping late. My mom ended up moving to the same community as my grandma, and she wasn't fond of it. My mom knew that living in the same community as my grandma guaranteed visitors from her siblings whenever they were in the neighborhood. She didn't like anyone popping up on her. It was bad enough that she was about to move into an apartment again. Once my mom got her apartment situated, we went shopping. We both tried on clothes in the dressing room, but when we approached the mirror, my mom became frustrated. She threw the clothes on the floor and stormed out of the store. I followed behind her, suggesting she just buy a size smaller. My mom yelled that the pants were already a size 0. The store clerks gave us confused looks, so I just threw my hands up. I felt helpless to my mom.

Tax season came around and everyone at school and in the neighborhood was wearing new fits, shoes, and fresh hairdos. I could identify the have and have-nots almost instantly. People who weren't accustomed to the material lifestyle had new attitudes: The constant attention-seeking behaviors, Students who you didn't even notice in class suddenly needed frequent bathroom breaks, interruptions in the classroom to sharpen a pencil, and let's not neglect to add the yelling across the cafeteria. People who were usually quiet began to taunt the same people with whom they were associated. My mom bought me new things during tax season sometimes, but not that year. We had a rough year. My mom had just moved, so all our tax money went on bills. I wasn't upset because Angel did my hair in some cute, blonde, and black individual braids with curls on the end. If my hair was done, I was good, and I didn't care who had something to say. Angel's brother was hosting another party at Club Bankhead, and she wanted me to go with her. The Rich Kidz was performing their new album titled, *Straight like That*. Rich Kidz were famous rappers to everyone else, but they were our peers and our friends. We attended school with the lead rapper, Skool boy. Angel got money from her mom, but I was broke. She suggested getting our nails done before the party.

It was a Friday night, and my mom came in drunk from my uncle's party. I tiptoed in her room as she was sound asleep. Once I got close to her, she turned over and made a moaning sound. I swiftly squatted to the floor because I couldn't afford to get caught. I crawled to her jeans that she had worn and checked the pockets. It was only a twenty-dollar bill in one pocket and nothing in the others. I crawled out the door and called Angel. I told her I only had twenty dollars and she said that it was cool because we were getting in the club for free. Angel and I went to City nails at Downtown Atlanta and got full sets for $15. I had just enough money to get my nails done and catch the bus. Bus fare was $1.75. We dressed over at Angel's aunt's house, and Angel's sister was talking about going to the mall. I heard Angel talking to another one of our classmates in the hallway at school earlier that day about going to the mall, but I didn't catch the whole conversation. Angel's sister's friend was a booster, and she was going to the mall with us. Angel's sister wasn't going in because she was the driver. She had paid her friend to steal for her.

When we entered the mall, the first store was Dillard's. Angel and I walked around looking at things, separating ourselves from her sister's friend. The girl walked in with empty shopping bags to disguise herself as a regular shopper. The bags were also used to fill with stolen clothing. As we walked around, I started asking questions because I knew I didn't have Dillard's money. Angel informed me that we needed to look out for her sister's friend. No one had told me that part. I felt nervous about the whole thing and

Chapter Six—GRACE

my palms started to get sweaty. As we walked around touching things and buying nothing, a woman came around and asked if we needed assistance. We both replied, "no," at the same time. I started feeling nervous and Angel warned me that I looked suspicious, so I took a deep breath to try to calm down. As we approached the dressing room, the girl gave us clothes and kept walking. I just looked because I was confused. Angel said, "Hurry up and put this on under your clothes." "Why, for what?" I asked. "Girl, don't you want to be fresh tonight?" "Just put it on under your clothes and look normal." I swiftly grabbed the bag and put the clothes on as best as I could; The Ralph Lauren shirt with horses all over and the jeans to match. I was much smaller than Angel and the pants I had on already had room in them, so it worked out. When we walked out of the dressing room, I remembered that my Rock-a-wear clutch was missing. I alarmed Angel. We both looked at one another in awe and sighed. "Girl, where do you last remember it? We got to go," Angel stated. "I don't know; I think I left it when that lady came talking to us," I replied. We looked around and couldn't find my clutch anywhere, so I decided to just leave it. We noticed Angel's sister's friend heading towards the exit, so we rushed towards the exit as calmly as possible. The girl slipped right out of the door as we were approached by two security guards. "May we check your bags please, ladies?".

 My heart started beating out of my chest. I thought about running, but then I thought about getting caught again. "Come with me, please," said the mall cop. One guard walked with Angel, and the other walked with me. We were put in separate rooms in the back of the mall where we were questioned. I didn't admit to anything and informed them that they missed the booster walking out the door by a second. I was left in the room alone for a minute until the lady walked in with my clutch. She saw us the whole time. "You were so busy trying to steal that you lost your business," she teased. I felt so stupid that all I could do was listen. That wasn't even the worst part. She asked me to take off the merchandise from under my clothes. At that moment, I wished I was invisible. I undressed and dressed in my regular clothes. Then, I was allowed to enter the hallway where Angel and I reunited. We shook our heads at each other as we were escorted into another room. We were asked to call our parents. I knew my mom would curse me out, and she would never let me live that moment down, but I also didn't trust anyone else. My mom answered the phone. "Ma, I need you to come get me from the mall," I pleaded. My mom didn't know the situation, so she just told me to catch the bus. "I'm in trouble," I disclosed. "In trouble? Adore, what the fuck were you up there doing?" she asked. "Stealing," I responded. "So that is what you do? You steal now? You need to sit your ass down." I gave the phone to the mall cops. Angel and I waited outside the mall. Then, I saw Angel's mom approaching with someone else. It was my big sister. They both arrived at the same time. I felt a big sigh of relief come over me. We told them the truth about the whole thing. Then, I told my sister the lie that I wanted her to tell my mom, so I could still go to the party. My mom called my sister to get an update. My sister told her exactly what we rehearsed. My mom asked to speak with me and gave me this whole lecture about not being a follower and how the follower always get the worst punishment because they are the most misinformed.

Soon as I was about to step out of the car, my mom called, yelling at me, saying I had stolen $100 from her. I told her that I only found twenty dollars on the floor. She asked my whereabouts, and I let her know that I was with Angel. She called me a liar and a thief and hung up in my face. I downplayed the whole conversation to Angel, who was waiting for me to take her picture outside of the club. I just told her my mom called to check on me.

Chapter Six—GRACE

The party was jumping, as usual. All the local cliques were there, and it was tax season, so everybody was fresh and in stunt mode. When we left the club, Angel said we were spending the night on Simpson Road. I was shocked because I already knew she meant that we were staying with some boys, and that area was known to be gang-infested. I told Angel I didn't want to be around those boys in their territory because anything could happen, and we'd be stranded. Angel brushed it off and told me that I was tripping. She knew them, but I only heard the rumors about them. We stayed in the dark the whole time and used our phones for light. It was the weirdest sleepover ever, but I already knew what type of environment I was headed to before I agreed to go. I prayed so hard before I went because even though I was bold most of the time, I always feared something tragic happening to me while being at the wrong place at the wrong time. The boys were cool, though, mostly cracking jokes the whole night. I was playing it cool but thinking "never again" the whole time. My mom called me early in the morning and told me to "bring my thieving ass home."

When I got home, my mom was cleaning and cooking Sunday dinner. She started talking about the money as soon as she saw me. "You took way more than $20," she scolded me. "You got nails and all that shit." I clarified again that I found $20, and I got a full set at city nails with it and used the rest for bus fare. I walked off and she was still talking to herself. I still heard her from upstairs faintly, "What got you wanting to steal? Your ass gone end up in jail; keep playing."

My mom desperately wanted to move from Dogwood Apartments. She said there were too many kids in the neighborhood. We ended up staying there for less than a year. The lease wasn't even expired before we were out and on to the next. My mom asked my sister to stay in the apartment to keep it from being broken into, and she agreed. That didn't last a week before my mom stopped by and caught my sister's baby dad there and put him out. She said she didn't want to enable them, and all my sister had to do was look out for herself and lay low. We moved into an old brick house that was painted a dark, greyish color. My mom was familiar with our neighbors already. She knew a man across the street from childhood. The next-door neighbor was the candy lady, who also sold beer, shots, and cigarettes. There were always parties next door, and my mom would attend them sometimes.

Angel came to visit me, and she wanted to spend the night because her mom was incarcerated. My mom allowed her to spend the night, but when she wanted to stay longer, my mom disapproved. I already knew that my mom would say no, so I asked Angel to ask her. Angel had more flexibility in her life. I could stay over at her house any day of the week, but my mom didn't play that. Initially, I didn't share Angel's business with my mom, but after she declined to let her stay over, I did. Nothing changed. I thought that my mom would understand and extend some compassion because she could relate to Angel's situation. When my mom was incarcerated, Angel's mom didn't ask me any questions; she just treated me with kindness. Although Angel wasn't raised by her mom and her mom had issues, she accepted her mother's love whenever she expressed it. I understood. I could relate. Several times when my mom was locked up, I cried to Angel, and she consoled me. I bawled my eyes out whenever my mom went away. Angel internalized her pain. She liked to laugh and entertain. She would distract herself by always being on the move. I saw her like no one else could. Most people only appreciated her for her style and material possessions.

When Angel asked my mom to stay over again. My mom turned her face up and said, "No, Adore has school tomorrow." Then, she

Chapter Six—GRACE

accused her of being gay and liking me. She did not say it to her face, but she said it to me, and I was disgusted. When my older brother visited us that day, they both sat in the living room, gossiping about Angel. My brother made a comment about the way Angel dressed, and my mom interjected, "like a prostitute." Angel overheard the conversation and ran past them and out the front door. My mom seemed nonchalant and continued to talk about Angel. My brother and mom called me in the living room and attempted to give me a lecture about how important it was to choose the right friends. My brother didn't mean any harm. He was just going by the information that my mom had given him. I was taken back by the whole occurrence. I ran outside to find Angel. I walked around the neighborhood and checked all the bus stops. I couldn't find her. I walked back home. My brother was gone. I knew how it felt to have a heavy heart but was constantly on the move. Running away from home had never crossed my mind. I valued my privacy too much. My sister didn't make it seem fun either, but that day I was hurt. I was tired of being misunderstood. My mom was in the kitchen cooking with music playing. I grabbed her phone and slipped out of the door. I called Nya and told her everything. I told her that I was on the way and to meet me at the bus stop. When I got off the bus, the sun had set. Nya informed me that I had to sneak in because she didn't tell her mom I was coming over. As we were walking to her house from the bus stop, the phone started ringing. I knew it was my mom. I didn't answer. She called again and again. Then, she left a voicemail. My mom and I shared her phone, so I knew the code to the voicemail. I checked the voicemail, and my mom was calm. She asked me to bring the phone back and told me I could stay if I wanted to and to just give her the phone back. Then, she called again. I was still scared to answer. Nya and I walked in and her mom was standing at the door. "Where is she coming from?" She asked. "You didn't ask to have company," she added. Nya covered me and told her mom that I had just gotten off the bus and I was only staying for a second. We walked to her room and the notification banner displayed that my mom had left another voicemail. She was upset and warned me that if she didn't get that phone back that night, she would report me as a runaway. I knew she wasn't bluffing. I told Nya to walk outside with me while I called her back. She alerted her mom that we were going to sit on the porch. I called my mom back. She asked for Nya's address so she could come get the phone. We looked around and gave her an address way down the street from Nya's house. I knew better than to give my mom Nya's address. I knew my mom would make a scene and Nya's mom had no clue what was happening.

I saw my stepdad's car approaching and tossed the phone to Nya and hid behind a truck that was parked on the side of the street. My mom got out of the car and grabbed the phone from Nya. I didn't expect her to get out of the car. I got scared and got under the truck so that she couldn't see me. She asked Nya where she lived, and Nya pointed her in the opposite direction. "You better not be lying," my mom threatened. When Larry drove off, I came from under the truck, and Nya and I ran to her house as quickly as we could. Nya snuck me in that night, but I left right after her mom went to work, around 7:00am. I reunited with Angel in Dogwood apartments. She was her usual happy self. We recalled all the events of the time we had last seen one another. She said that she had been with her cousin. I was relieved to know that she was doing well, and I ended up going back to her cousin's house with her for a while. They were getting ready to go to the movies, so Angel and I decided to catch a ride to her aunt's house. My mom called and demanded I come home. I showered as soon as I got in. Then, my mom and I discussed the events leading to me running away. She still expressed her doubts about me and Angel's friendship, but I didn't even bother to argue with her about it.

Chapter Six—GRACE

The next day at school, I met up with Jade in the hallway. She was talking to me about some girls who had been bothering her on the bus. I knew of the siblings because they lived next door to Nya, but I didn't know the friend she was referring to. Jade turned my attention to the girl who happened to be in the distance. When the girl and I caught eyes, she made it known that she would "get on Jade's head" and threatened to fight me too if I wanted to be in it. Jade was about to say something back to her, but I persuaded her not to argue. I was sitting in my computer class when I overheard my name a few rows ahead of me. I looked up, and it was one of my close guy friends chatting with the girl Jade had issues with. I had never seen her in my class. He attempted to defend me, but he really escalated the situation. When he told her that I could fight, she got loud and said, "I don't care; she can't beat me, though." My teacher stood up at her desk and asked her to leave. My classmates informed the teacher that she wasn't even supposed to be in our class. When the bell rang, my friend tapped me on the shoulder and said, "beat her ass." I didn't intend to fight anyone. I didn't want Jade to fight either.

The hallway was full of students talking and transitioning to classes. I was headed to the gym when I ran into Jade. She was upset. She was talking fast, explaining that the older sister of the two siblings kept making smart remarks towards her. Just to our surprise, the younger sibling was walking up the steps where we were standing. The girl and Jade began to argue. I grabbed Jade and pulled her away and the girl attacked Jade from behind. The crowd circled around the fight. The older sister and her friend jumped in as well. I moved through the crowd and tapped the girl who called me out on the shoulder. She turned around, and I punched her in the face. The girl and I fell to the floor. I was on top, and she was holding my shirt so tight that it ripped off. I kicked the girl until she released my shirt. The fight was two against three.

Everyone declared that Jade and I had won. I had blacked out. I didn't hear or see anyone around me. All I heard were faint voices. I came back to reality when my teacher grabbed me and escorted me to his classroom. I didn't even notice my shirt was off until he told me.

The other girls were escorted to the office by the assistant principal, but my teacher spared me when he guided me back to his classroom. Therefore, I didn't get caught with the other girls. I put my jacket on and sat on top of the desk. I became anxious as I was reenacting the scenario that led to the fight. My teacher commended me for standing up for myself. He suggested that I remained calm and didn't go to the office unless they sent for me. Every girl on the senior hall had a crush on Mr. Muhammad. He was 6 feet tall, Muslim, light-skinned, and had a New Orleans accent. He was always smooth, even when he had to redirect someone who was disruptive in the classroom. They probably fantasized about being alone with him, but I had gained a newfound respect for him.

Chapter Seven
ONE OF MANY

My sister and the kids came to live with us temporarily. Patience had gotten big, but our bond was the same. It felt so good to be in the same house again. My sister began dating a guy she met in the community. We found out about it because he was my older brother's age, and my brother knew of him. Everyone on the block was talking about their relationship. Everyone was teasing the guy, saying that my sister was only with him to get his social security check. My mom nor my brother approved of the relationship. My mom attended a gathering at our next-door neighbor's house. We didn't see her until the morning after. She woke up upset because my nephew had been crying all night. She barged into the room and told my sister that she had to leave because the baby was too loud. My sister barely had her eyes open when my mom attempted to grab the baby from the bed. My sister jumped up and yelled, "Don't pull my baby by his arm." My sister and mom argued back and forth about whether my mom pulled my nephew by his arm or not. "Adore, did I pull him by his arm?" My mom asked. "Yes," I replied. My mom was furious at that point and grabbed my niece and walked her towards the door. "Adore, you can get the fuck out too," she yelled. My sister grabbed my nephew, and I followed my mom with the double stroller. My sister and I stood outside in the summer heat as my mom yelled from the window for us to get away from her porch. My sister argued that she needed the rest of her things. My mom called the police on us, but she didn't come out of the house to speak with them.

When the police arrived, my sister recalled the whole scenario, and the policeman screened my mom's information. "She has a warrant," he said. I put my head in my hand. The policeman knocked on the door and asked my mom to come out. "This isn't about me sir, I want them off of my property," she responded. "Ma'am, you have a warrant. I need you to come out," the officer ordered. My mom opened the door and came out a few moments later. As she entered the police car, she made it known that she wanted her house locked down. The policeman informed us that he had to call family and children services if we didn't have a family member to come get us off the property. We called my aunts and my brother's dad. My brother's dad arrived first, and my little brother was gone. My aunts arrived and started yelling at us, saying we were going to stress their sister into an early grave. One of my aunts called us hot pussy hoes and my sister started defending us until she couldn't take it anymore. She locked her babies in the stroller and left. My sister had left just in time because family and children services pulled in the driveway seconds later. They had missed her only by a few seconds. I was the only one left. The social worker said that I had to go with them. My aunt suggested that I go with her, but the worker specified that because DFCS were called on the scene, I had to come with her. I didn't say anything. I just followed the Social Worker. My thoughts were so crowded with how fast everything had happened.

The Social Worker was kind to me. She didn't say much, but she stopped by McDonald's and bought me a meal. She adjusted the temperature in the car because I told her that I was cold. I never even thought to ask her where I was going. We arrived at the brick building. When we entered the lobby, there were other kids there. That is when the Social Worker told me that we would be parting ways. I questioned what would happen to me. She introduced me to another person and told me they would explain things to me. The other Social Worker spoke with me about finding a placement until I get to go back home to my mom. I watched as the room became emptier with fewer kids until finally, the worker came back for me. We got in her car and drove to the Camp Creek area. The house was big and gated. The door opened and there stood an older, black woman. The Social Worker acquainted the foster mom and me and left. As soon as the worker left, the foster mom introduced me to her family, who were sitting on the couch in the dining area a few feet from the entrance of the home. Then, she put me on display and asked me to tell them what had happened. "My mom went to jail; that's why I'm here," I said, walking away. My foster parent proceeded to fill in the details. Then, she showed me around the house and told me to make myself at home. When I was shown where I would be sleeping, I was greeted by a set of twins who were also in foster care. The twins and I walked to the park and became acquainted. I learned that their mom had passed from a drug overdose. They also shared with me that they were in the custody of their aunt, but she was just a money-hungry leech using them for their check and not adequately supporting them. Their story changed my mindset about my situation. I began to miss my mom. Prior to meeting the twins, I had a personal conversation with my foster mom. My foster mom and her family were actually very kind to me. She just wanted to get to know me so that she could understand me. I shared with her that I liked to read and that I valued my education. She, in return, told me that if I aged out of the foster care system that I was guaranteed admission into college, paid for by the state. Then, I was informed that the state provided $300 shopping sprees for my clothing every so often. She allowed me to use the phone, and I called Nya. Her number was the only number I knew. She didn't know who I was. She said the caller ID read, "unknown caller." She was baffled that I had been placed in the system. I made her promise not to tell anyone. My mom didn't stay incarcerated for long. My caseworker tried to reclaim my clothing, but my mom told them off. I wasn't surprised when I was told about that because I knew how my mom felt about the system.

The morning of my court date, my foster mom prepared me for court. She was a cosmetologist. She commented that my hair didn't need relaxers. She offered to treat my hair and get it to grow healthy. She shampooed, pressed, and clipped my ends. I felt so confident with my hair pressed, although it was short. She told me that I had a bright future ahead of me and that she'd see me after court. I appreciated her, and I liked her, but I didn't tell her that I was hoping to God that I would be going home after court. My mom didn't show up to court. The judge was disgusted, and I thought that my life as I knew it was over until the judge called my mom on the speakerphone. My mom answered and told the judge that she had mistaken the court date and she wanted me to come home. The relief I felt was indescribable. I was transported home by the same social worker who picked me up. My mom wasn't happy to see me like I expected. She asked me how I ended up in foster care and inquired about my hair. Supposedly, my aunt told her I chose to go with the Social Worker. I wasn't surprised that my aunts blamed me for being in foster care, but I think my mom was more humiliated than anything. Regardless of what my mom did, she always upheld her invincible demeanor, and she hated for people to be in her business unless she told it. When she caused damage, she would apologize and expect it to erase the pain forever.

My mom found a brick house for rent on the street over from that house, and it was a much calmer environment for the most part. The street that we previously lived on had much more activity due to our neighbor being the candy lady and the man across the street renovating his home. I became acquainted with a girl down the road and came to find out that she knew my sister. She and my big sister were close friends. She was also a hairstylist, and that is how we became cool. She did my hair and started calling me her little sister until she started dating a local guy. At first, she was so into him that if he called while she was doing my hair, she would do a rush job just so she could see him. I guess that was the honeymoon phase. Then, their relationship became toxic because she found out he was with his baby mom. When they started physically fighting and arguing a lot, I stayed away for a while. I invited Nya over and my mom made it known that she didn't like her and never wanted to see her face again. Nya just laughed. I didn't understand why my mom held a grudge for Nya. Nya was only doing what any real friend would do.

I couldn't take the boredom any longer. At our new house, I was always alone. Empress didn't stay far, so I started visiting her more. We would watch TV and eat snacks at her house or walk to the park. She was still crazy about Derrick's nephew, but she was dating other people. Honestly, I was happy to hear that. It never mattered how long we didn't talk; Empress and I loved each other the same. I considered Empress to be a loyal friend. I never questioned her loyalty or love for me, and her energy was always refreshing. I admired how she cared for her siblings and assisted her mom. Empress talked about the things she wanted to do after high school, but she rebutted and stated that she didn't want to go too far from her mom. I respected her for that, but I knew that If I was presented the opportunity, I would leave.

My sister and my mom had beef after my mom's release. I don't know what escalated, but my sister came by the house and knocked over the mailbox. I came into the house and my mom was leaving her a nasty voicemail threatening to put a warrant out on her. I just walked past her and went to my room. Later that evening, my aunt came over and hung out with my mom. When she saw my hair, she immediately asked my mom if she could fix it. My aunt had been a beautician since the '80s. She slayed my hair once, so I trusted her. My mom gave her a few dollars to buy my weave. She purchased two packs of blonde bundles and some needles and thread. I was known to wear blonde hair. She gave me a full sewin with a bang. She slanted my bang because she said slanted bangs were in, but I had never seen anyone with a slanted bang. My hair was still cute to me, crooked bangs and all. I didn't even try to adjust it. I just knew I was fine when I went to school the next day. Everybody was asking who had done my hair. I stayed after-school with my dance friends. I had joined the hip-hop dance group at school, and most of my friends were in the group.

When I got home, my mom was in a good mood, but I could tell she had been drinking. My sister called my phone just to check in on me, so our conversation was brief. She just asked what I was doing and what I had been up to, and I asked her the same questions. As soon as we hung up, my mom walked into the living room. She asked who I was on the phone with, but she already knew. She had never expressed suspicion about my phone conversations before, so I just stood, staring at her, perplexed. "I told you not to talk to her in my house," she said, walking towards me. I tried to move and hit my hip on the deep freezer. That is when my mom reached for the phone, and it fell out of my hand and onto the floor. I stormed out of the house, yelling, "I'm tired of this shit." Then I kicked the green garbage bin over. My mom immediately called the police. By the time the police arrived, things had calmed down, but I was still on the porch. My mom explained to the policeman that things were fine, but the policeman commanded that someone come with him. I looked at my mom, and she looked at me. "You go, Adore, I'll come get you," she reassured. The ride felt awkward and silent until the policeman broke the ice. "I hate to have to do this to you," he alleged. "Well, don't, drop me off at my friend's house," I asserted. "I already called it in, so I have to take you to the station," he claimed. I honestly felt nothing. I had no feeling, not even apprehension. Waiting in the station, I began to feel anxious. It was getting late, and I wanted to go home.

When I arrived at the metro juvenile facility, reality had sunk in, but I was still in disbelief. I started to reflect on everything that transpired over the previous months. I was in a daze when I was called to the clinic. The two nurses examined me and asked if the sew-in was my real hair. I told the truth. The nurse said I should've said yes because I had to take it out. I gasped in disappointment and explained to them that I had just gotten my hair done. They complimented my hair and agreed to let me keep my hair in for that night. "You have court tomorrow?" One of the nurses asked. "Yes," I replied. The nurse alerted me that after court, if I didn't go home, I would have to take my hair out because it wasn't allowed. I sighed in relief because I knew I was going home. I slept in a small room until the next morning.

I was awakened by the loud door opening and a JCO yelling my last name for the court. No one was in the courtroom but the judge, juvenile intake officers, and me. I looked around for my mom as I thought that maybe they had to invite her in like the court cases on television. She didn't show up. The judge ordered that I stay for 12 days to teach me a lesson. I felt lost and betrayed. I had finals the following week. I had been studying for weeks. Tears filled my eyes, and I couldn't stop crying.

As I sat waiting for whatever would come next, I noticed another young lady sitting ahead of me. She was bawling her eyes out just like me. We both were stunned by the disturbance in the distance and looked up. A young lady was fighting the officers escorting her. It took three officers to reprimand her. The other girl and I locked eyes, I shook my head at her, and we both began to cry again. A 6 foot tall JCO with short hair came and escorted me to an empty room. She told me to take all my clothes off. I paused and waited for her to leave the room as I undressed. She proceeded to tell me to squat and cough. I couldn't help but think that it was some sick game she was playing, but the look on her face was serious. I quickly did a half squat and coughed. She gave me a death stare, walked over, and closed the once cracked door. "Listen here, I don't have time for your attitude. I got some nieces back there that will beat your little ass," she made known. I tried to compose myself from the intimidation that she imposed on me. "This is my first time here; I didn't know," I replied. "It's ok, swat lower and cough so that I know you have no weapons." I did just that. She sprayed my hair with a strong-smelling solution and gave me enough soap to bathe a newborn baby. She handed me all blue clothing and slides. I grabbed the panties and held them up to my face. I noticed that they were recycled and not new before I even noticed that they were large. "We are out of smalls. We will get your size later," she disclosed.

I went back to sit with the girl I had seen earlier. We introduced ourselves. She told me that her mom reported her as a runaway because she didn't like her older boyfriend. In her judgment, he was a good person and wasn't causing her any harm. I found comfort in talking to her. We became cool. I shared with her why I was there. We talked and hung out during recreation. Everyone was gay for the stay in Juvie. I didn't think it was cute or funny. One girl started calling me sis. She was cool at first. She even braided my hair after the lady who usually fixed hair didn't show up. Then, I quickly learned that "sis" was the gateway to becoming someone's girlfriend. I didn't have any trouble in there besides the gay for the stay mess. One of the girls who called me her sis made a hand gesture that made me uncomfortable, so I had to make a scene. We were in the day room where all the girls sat and watched T.V when we weren't on lockdown. I set her straight in front of everyone. I told her to miss me with the gay shit; I don't go that way. All the girls just stared at us. The girl was a dark skin, short stud with a feminine voice. She wore her hair in a short, natural afro, but she could really fix some hair. There was no bad blood between us after that. She just laughed it off.

My days were becoming weary in Juvie. I was tired of being locked down. I hated the toilet being in my room with me and the bed being so close to the wall. The room was so disgusting to me. I created fantasies in my head when we were locked down just so I wouldn't have to think. When I did think, I cried. I hated that I was missing school. I felt like I was wasting my life away. On my court date, I was shackled on my wrists and my ankles. I couldn't believe myself. I was in the back of a van with other girls who had court. They were conversing. I was lost in my thoughts. "I'll never allow this to happen again," was my final thought. I finally saw my mom in the courtroom after two long weeks. We barely locked eyes because the judge was questioning her. The judge questioned my mom about my character. My mom spoke highly of me. "Well, why is she here? How are her grades?" The judge inquired. "She does well in school; it's when she's home," my mom responded. The judge ordered that I be evaluated before returning home. When we approached the desk to fill out the paperwork, my mom asked if I wanted to go through with the evaluation. "You could get a check," she apprised. I disapproved, and she retracted, "yeah fuck that shit let's go." She pushed the paper back on the desk and we left. My mom embraced me and apologized once we were outside. She expressed that she couldn't even recognize me when she saw me in that courtroom. "What happened to your hair?" She asked. I explained to her the whole process. "You don't even look like yourself; that place is not for you," she expressed before apologizing again.

Once I returned to school, my friends asked where I had been. I showed everyone my black and white mug shot which was cut out in a laminated piece of paper. I recalled the occurrence I had with the Juvenile corrections officer. Queen couldn't get enough. She laughed hysterically and called me over to tell others about it, but no one laughed as hard as her. My sister had been calling my phone when I was in juvenile. She had also been in contact with my older brother when I was away. They both wanted to know where I had been. My sister found out from one of my schoolmates that I had been in Juvenile. My sister called to confront my mom and my mom denied everything. My older brother also called and had a conversation with my mom. He declared to my mom that she shouldn't call the police on me anymore because I could become accustomed to that lifestyle and be just like my sister. My mom listened and agreed. She confided in my brother that she realized the impact that juvenile had on me and that she and I established an understanding.

My little brother got in an incident with a local guy down the street. The guy was the boyfriend of the girl I used to hang out with, who I called my sister. He slapped my little brother in the face and left a handprint. I was in the house studying when my little brother walked into my room. "Adore, your friend's boyfriend slapped me," he said, turning his jaw towards me. I immediately became furious. "He slapped you hard; he left a handprint on your face." I leaped off the bed. "Calm down, don't tell Ma. It's ok," he muttered. "Boy, stop, that's a grown-ass man; he has no business putting his hands on you," I snapped. My brother claimed the guy was just playing, but I was not hearing that. I called my mom, and she didn't answer, but she walked in shortly afterward. I rushed to her and bombarded her with information. She looked at my brother's face and called my brother's dad. They were both on the phone yelling back and forth until he said he was on the way. My brother's dad pulled up and my mom and brother walked down to the guy's house and confronted him. The guy insisted that he was just playing with my little brother. My mom made it known that she was taking him to court and that he could tell it to the judge. The guy acted nonchalantly as if he did nothing wrong. For days, it appeared as if nothing was happening. My old friend started to show up at my house again, but my mom warned that she was an informant for the dude. She told me not to share anything and just say I don't know if she asks me anything. My brother's dad was a veteran. He was observant than anything. He was more about action. My mom did take the guy to court and the guy was arrested. As far as everyone was concerned, we were newcomers, and he was family. My brother's dad always brought his guns when he came over just in case. The tension on the street became thick. It felt strange just walking past my neighbors' homes to catch the school bus.

Chapter Eight

NEW BEGINNINGS

My mom eventually found a nice brick house in the Collier Heights community. The area was familiar to me because my school bus picked up and dropped off in the neighborhood. I liked the interior of that house the most, but it was one of the most short-term houses we had ever resided in. Most of my neighbors were either acquaintances or my classmates. Although it was technically not a new area, I didn't make friends. Everyone had their pacts. Most of the residents were family. One of my elementary school friends invited me to her birthday celebration. I hadn't seen her since her family moved away from the westside of Atlanta. Jamie and I were the top students of our 4th-grade class, and we were best friends. Facebook kept us connected after she moved away. Our lives were obviously different, so I was intrigued by invitation. I didn't allow any barriers to prevent me from showing up.

I called Chris to take me to Jamie's dinner. When I arrived, everyone was already seated, and food was being passed around. Jamie had already called and gotten my order over the phone. She introduced me to her friends, we ate our food and engaged in good conversation. Later that night, we played "never have I ever," which led to other good conversations. I liked her friends. They were supportive. Jamie's best friend had called to invite me to her celebration. I thought that was so cute. It was like Jamie had her own entourage. I had planned to attend the dinner party, stay the night, and leave the next morning. The next day, we cooked breakfast together and hung out around the house. I was texting

Chris the whole time, trying to secure my ride back home. Chris was an older guy. I met him through Tia one night when I was put out. He picked me up with Tia on the passenger side. He would take us wherever we needed to go, buy us food, and whatever else we needed. I told Jazz that I was leaving & she insisted that I stay for the rest of her festivities. I let her know that I didn't bring anything else to wear because I wasn't aware of anything more. I told her that my ride may not be available to take me home the next day either. Jamie offered to find me something to wear and to take me home. I felt so appreciated and important like my presence meant something. We ransacked her room, got dressed and eventually left. Jazz drove her mom's car. We were supposed to attend a pool party of one of their guy friends, but we arrived too late. We ended up taking pictures in the parking lot and just chatting with the guys until one of them mumbled something that was disrespectful. I didn't catch what he said, but the disgust on the other girl's face said enough. The next morning, we all ate cereal and chatted. That is when I was introduced to what the guy had said. He asked if we were there to have sex. His delivery was much more provocative. Gradually, the other ladies left, and Jamie and I were alone. We talked to each other to sleep, literally. It was so funny because it reminded me of how we had to be separated in elementary school because we talked too much. We would always get called out for talking. We just had so much to catch up on. We talked mostly about our peers and our education.

When Jazz pulled up at my house, I didn't expect her to want to go inside, but she wanted to speak to my mom. My mom didn't answer the phone when I called to tell her I was on the way, so I wasn't even sure she was home. Prior to visiting Jamie, I was staying over at Tia's house. Surprisingly, the door was already open, so I just turned the knob and we walked in. As we walked past the kitchen, I noticed that my mom had all four of the stove

Chapter Eight—NEW BEGINNINGS

burners lit and the oven door open. I glimpsed and Jamie noticed as well. I quickly went into the kitchen and turned everything off. "I don't know why that was on," I uttered. "To keep the house warm, girl," Jamie responded.

I knocked on my mom's door and she invited me to her room. I informed her that Jamie wanted to speak to her. I didn't know if she'd remember her from elementary, but she did. My mom hugged Jamie and complimented her on her beauty. She also told her to come over whenever she'd like. We walked Jamie out, and my mom saw Jamie's mom's Mercedes Benz backed in the driveway. "That's Jamie's car, Adore?" "No, that's her mom's car; she's waiting inside," I replied. "She got her some money and moved out the hood," my mom added. When she walked past the kitchen, she noticed that I had turned everything off. She burst out laughing and said, "You turned that shit off." I let her know that I felt embarrassed and asked why she had all the burners on in the Summer. She said it was cold and the central heat took too long to warm the house. We eventually left that house due to an ant infestation. We tried every affordable remedy to help the situation, but nothing worked. The ants were everywhere, especially the bathroom. My last day at that place was one that I'd never forget. I had just gotten home from Tia's place; it had just gotten dark outside and was beginning to rain.

When I entered the front door, I noticed my mom had moved everything that she could salvage to the living room and front room of the house. Everything was turned off in the house except the living room television. It was difficult to find ample walk space. My mom was dozing off, so I tipped past her and went into the front room to search for a change of clothes. My mom mumbled something, but I couldn't hear her clearly. I just continued digging in the clothes hamper. My mom got up and leaned over some of the things on the floor. "Turn that light off, "she asserted. "I'm looking for something right quick," I replied. I don't give a damn turn that light off," she said, walking towards the bathroom. I quickly turned the light off and mumbled under my breath. My mom heard me and started going in about how I always must get the last word. I didn't understand why she was so upset with me. I sighed in confusion and sat in the dark with the clothes on my lap. My mom lost her temper and told me to "get the fuck out." "No, it's about to storm out there," I stated. "You are getting the fuck out of here," my mom said, approaching me. My mom marched me right out the front door with no shoes on. I banged on the door, yelling, "I don't have any shoes on. Please give me shoes, it's raining". My mom cracked the door and tossed some flats at me. For a while, I was quiet because I didn't know where I was even supposed to go. Then, I started banging on the door again. I didn't get a response. I started banging and yelling, "Ma, it's raining, I'm sorry." "Let me back in, please." I didn't get a response. I tapped on the window and the glass shattered. I was so shocked I hopped off on the porch towards the street. It was not my intention to break the window. My adrenaline was racing. Moments later, my mom opened the door. "I'm about to call the police on your ass," she made known.

I started walking, then jogging, then running. The rain was getting heavier. All I was thinking was I couldn't let the police see me. I didn't even have a location in mind until I reached the main road. It was dark. I started praying. I prayed that my mom didn't alert the police. I prayed that no one would abduct me. I started reciting, "I rebuke the devil in the name of Jesus" repeatedly. I headed toward Angel's house. Angel's house was only a 5-minute drive, but it was a 30-minute walk. The rain did not let up. My flats were so soaked, I was practically walking barefoot. I started to cry. Then I wiped my eyes. I had the sniffles. When I reached the main road of Angel's community, a car passed me and then pulled over.

Chapter Eight—NEW BEGINNINGS

I caught up to the car. A young guy with short dreadlocks offered me a ride. I stood and stared for a second. "I'm good," I assured. "Shawty, you are wet and shit. I don't want to leave you out here," he responded. He put the car back in drive. "I'm just going right around the corner," I said as I opened the car door. I pointed towards Angel's Street. I instructed the guy to drop me off a little way up the street from Angel's house. When we pulled up, I thanked him and considered him a good Samaritan until he uttered his next thought. "You ain't gone give me nothing shawty?" I put my hand on the door handle, opened the door, and peeped back at him. I said, "Give you what? I said thank you." "Some head or something," he responded, gesturing at his penis. "No!" I jumped completely out of the seat and cracked the door almost shut! He said OK and drove off. I ran to Angel's door and the door was open. Angel unlocked the screen door. She was with another girl that I knew from Bowen Homes. They were about to leave. I greeted them both and signaled Angel to come into her room with me. I just told her that my mom put me out and I had walked all the way to her house. She shook her head and took me out a change of clothes from her drawer. She put her pointer finger over her lip and gestured at the door. I shook my head in agreement.

I went back home, and my mom and I had a talk. I told her that I didn't intend to shatter the window. I just wanted to get back in the house. She informed me that she reported it as a burglary to the police so that the landlord could replace the window. She went on to say that we were moving away and that I would be transferring schools. I wasn't surprised that we were moving, but changing schools came as a shock. I wasn't sad or upset. I was curious more than anything. My mom had located a house on Creel Road in College Park. It was aesthetically different from our previous houses. It had a big backyard and a garage. It also had an open floor plan. We lived in a peaceful cul-de-sac, and a policeman was our next-door neighbor. After we settled in, my mom enrolled me in my new high school, and my first day wasn't bad at all. I didn't experience that gut-wrenching new student feeling. You know, when you're alone, and all eyes are on you so much that it makes you want to be invisible. When I entered my first class, I saw friendly faces. Several of my new classmates offered me a seat next to them. That made me feel welcomed. When I walked through the lunch line and got my tray, I knew I'd sit alone because I didn't have a crew like everyone else. To my surprise, I was offered a seat at a table by a girl named Parish. She called me a "pretty girl." I wasn't accustomed to those types of compliments from my peers at my old school. Then she asked my name. I introduced myself and shared that I had transferred from Douglas High school. "Oh, you from the Westside, y'all bad," one of the girls at the table implied. I laughed. I was shocked to see that they were so impressed that I was from the Westside. All the girls started talking to me at once. They were telling me about family and friends that they knew like the Westside was Beverly Hills or something. You would think that Fulton County was a tourist attraction. I sat in awe of them. Who knew that being raised in the hood was a flex? Banneker looked nothing like my previous high school, and the students were nicer. They weren't as flashy as my old peers except for a few. I stood out there. Even the guys found me to be attractive. At my old school, I was nothing more than a homegirl. I didn't have the name brands, so I wasn't considered top tier there. I didn't yearn to be popular, but it did feel good to be the big fish in the pond.

I met a shy girl that rode my school bus. I noticed her always standing alone at the bus stop while her two older sisters were always together. We became familiar one day when she sat by me on the school bus. After we became acquainted, I hung out with her. I invited her to my house, and I taught her to do makeup. She told me that her parents didn't allow her to wear make-up, but she

Chapter Eight—NEW BEGINNINGS

asked me to arch her eyebrows. When I saw her sisters at school, they confronted me about their sister's brows. They told me that I did good on her brows but that I got their little sister in trouble. I felt bad, and I learned a lesson that day. Everything is not for everybody, and just because my mom allowed me certain freedom does not mean that other parents had the same standards. I didn't even consider what that girl's parents would think about their daughter coming home looking different. Some of the students inquired about our friendship, boldly asking me why I hung out with her. I lied and told them that she was my cousin. I understood how it felt to be an outcast.

One day on our ride to school, my new friend confided in me that she was gay and that she had a crush on one of the girls that I had become cool with. I asked her if she made that known to the girl, and she said that it would be her first time ever approaching a girl and that she wasn't out yet. She also shared something with me that she said she was going to take to her grave. I was disturbed by our conversation, but it was an icebreaker. I felt that we had formed a bond from that day forward.

I developed close friendships with a couple real cool girls. What I liked the most about that school was the authenticity of everyone. I felt in my element. I could be myself, and people liked my personality and didn't gravitate towards me or seclude me because of the labels on my clothes. I started hanging out with a girl named Kya and started going over to her house after school. Her family was so hospitable, I became like family to them. I loved the person that I was becoming and my new environment. I loved my school, new friends, and new home. My mom seemed to be in a good place too. She bought both of us new phones. When I came home from school, she revealed the purple and white T-Mobile Comeback. It was love at first sight. I grabbed the phone and slid it up to reveal the keyboard. I hugged my mom tight enough to cut her circulation.

We visited the Westside every other Friday. My mom visited more often than that. I didn't care to visit as much, especially when I learned that Tia lived along the bus line. Tia lived about 15 minutes away. I started visiting her in Union City. Tia's mom moved to Union City when her projects were torn down. As soon as I walked in the door, Tia and I jumped up and down, hugging and screaming. I immediately noticed the long mirror on the wall at the entrance of the townhome and wanted us to snap a picture together. Tia's daughter came walking from the empty dining area. I grabbed her and squeezed her tight. Then, I spun her around. She laughed and I felt accomplished. Tia and I did a lot of catching up. My life was constantly changing, but besides the move, everything was the same with Tia. I expressed to her how blessed she was to have her mom support her with her daughter because Tia was able to come and go as she pleased. I talked to Tia about my new life with excitement and showed her my new friends on Facebook. She seemed genuinely happy for me, and she cracked a few jokes. My favorite thing about Tia was her humor. I was guaranteed some good laughs with Tia. Tia was a natural comedian, and being around her when I would go through hard times was like my medicine.

Being the new girl on the block brought a lot of attention to me, from the younger guys at school to the local, older guys in the community. I had a crush on this one guy at my school, but I quickly found out that he had a girlfriend. At the end of the school day, he caught our bus to her stop, and they would sit together on the bus. The funny thing is I came to know that he was from the Westside too. He stayed fresh and in the latest fashions, so I should've known. We spoke when we saw one another, and that was it. I ended up talking to the most unexpected guy. Parish, the first girl to become

Chapter Eight—NEW BEGINNINGS

my friend, was the one who suggested I give him a chance. "He's cool and respectful; give him a chance," she suggested. I saw Byron when I was leaving my JROTC class. We exchanged numbers in the hallway before the bell rang. Byron and I texted and talked on the phone regularly before he started staying over at his home boy's house on the weekends so that we could hang out. I would walk down to his homeboy house and Byron, and I would talk, play basketball, or curveball. I never went inside of his homeboy's house, no matter how many times Byron asked. I cared too much about my reputation. His friend already had a lot of brothers. There were just too many boys for me. One Saturday night, Byron called me late, around 12 am. I was chilling with my little brother. I wasn't going to answer, but I hadn't spoken with him all day. He wanted me to know that his phone was broken and that he had just arrived at his homeboy's house and got a new battery. Then, he asked me if I could meet him at the park. He added that he had snacks, and that tickled me. I had the phone on speaker and my little brother looked up and said, "let's go." I looked at him like he was crazy. I told Byron that I couldn't come because it was too late. We talked for a couple minutes and hung up. When I hung up, my little brother said he wanted to go to the park. "I'm bored and my daddy and Ma are sleeping," he pleaded. "Ok, but we not staying long," I affirmed. I couldn't believe what I was about to do. I called Byron back and told him that we would meet him at the park. When we arrived at the park, Byron was sitting on a bench with his backpack. He came off the bench and walked in the middle of the lit-up basketball court to hug me and greet my little brother. He opened his bag to show me the snacks. My little brother and I grabbed a fruit cup and walked back over to the bench with him. He was smiling from ear to ear. He pulled a basketball from under the bench, and he and my little brother started playing basketball. I started trying to play, and they were dunking and dribbling on me. Byron's phone rang, and he answered. He was telling his friends where he was and saying he was on the way back, so I ran and grabbed his backpack. His friends were coming to meet him halfway.

As we were walking down the road heading home, my little brother said, "Adore, there go mama and my daddy." "Swear to God," I replied. We were a few steps from a big, brick mailbox, so I suggested that we hide behind it. I went down first, and my brother dipped down too. Byron's friends were walking up the sidewalk. Byron was a few steps behind me. We were too late. We were exposed. My mom jumped out of the car before my brother's dad even came to a complete stop. "Bring y'all ass here, and I'm going to kill you!" she yelled. My little brother walked towards the car. My mom started slapping him in the head and everywhere else until he got into the car. It started drizzling, and I felt a raindrop hit my nose. I took off running and my mom started chasing me. Byron and his friends were cheering me on and laughing at the same time. My mom stopped and walked back to the car. "Bring your ass on," she demanded. She was asthmatic and out of breath. I got in the backseat of the car and my mom reached back and tried to hit me. She explained that she thought someone had kidnapped us and threatened that to beat me when we got in the house. She was almost out of breath when she asked for my phone and threw it out the window. I watched my phone fly out the window into the grass. I admit it was only at that point that I had any emotions about what I did. I knew that my mom had asthma and wouldn't beat me too bad. I felt like I could reason with her since she was already tired.

My brother's dad was the only barrier to getting through to my mom. My mom could be understanding when she wasn't influenced by anyone else. I don't know why my mom always felt the need to impress him in all that she did. Anytime my mom disciplined us, he'd continue to recall what happened, and they'd go on for hours like we weren't listening. It irritated me to hear his feedback.

Chapter Eight—NEW BEGINNINGS

Sometimes, I felt that my brother's dad thrived off negativity because he would be so passionate when we had drama in the house. He seldomly defended us when my mom was wrong. Ironically, he would churn out the truth when they had an argument just to be right. He was the only stepdad that I would claim, though. He raised us. He taught me things when he lived with us and was the sole disciplinarian when we were younger. He was fuel to her fire.

After he and my mom separated, things felt less tense in the house but more responsibility for my mom. I resented my stepdad for years because of all the changes we experienced. I tolerated him because my mom demanded that we respect him. She even forced me to call him daddy sometimes. He had another woman. He always had another woman, but it wasn't apparent to me until my mom started going to jail. What made me angry the most was how my mom treated him like a king when he came over. She wanted us to sleep when he came, so she'd rush us to help her clean while she cooked. Then she'd tell us to go to bed before he got there. She catered to him and still cheated with a woman with six kids, none of them by him. My mom told him all our business and wanted us to be admired by him. The other woman was the total opposite. She didn't cook for him. He ordered takeout. She wasn't stylish like my mom, but he still took her around his family. Her kids weren't nearly as well-mannered as we were, but he knew not to say anything derogatory about them in their mom's presence. He would be over at our house for days and then disappear on major holidays. My mom cooked well. He never needed Ruth Chris when he had a woman like my mom. She brought Ruth Chris to him. Yet, she still was the other woman. My mom didn't show sadness. She would keep her head up. I watched her call him plenty of times, leaving voicemails back-to-back. She'd say the nastiest things to try to hurt him for abandoning her. They played tug of war with each other's emotions. My little brother was not the focus, like my mom always claimed. She claimed to only keep my stepdad around because of my little brother. She said if she didn't act like she wanted him, she'd have to beg for him to pay child support. She constantly put him on child support and then took him off when they were on good terms. It wasn't my business until she would send me downtown to fill out the paperwork. Then I'd hear her cursing him out on his voicemail again about her putting him back on child support.

When we got in the house, my brother's dad called him into my mom's room. I walked straight to my room and prepared for my mom to walk in with an extension cord or something. I heard the door burst open, and I leaped off the bed. My mom was empty-handed. She sat down on the bed, and so did I. "I'm not going to hit you," she stated. She let me know that she knew that I wouldn't have taken my little brother with me if my intentions were to have sex. She told me that she was worried about us and made me promise to never do something like that again. I promised, and we hugged. Then, she said that my phone was probably ruined, but I could go get it if I knew where it landed. I ran outside and got my phone. The rain had gotten into it. It was water damaged. I heard my mom in the kitchen and showed her the phone. She gave me permission to use her phone with my sim card. I called Byron back, and he answered the phone on the first ring. He whispered, "I thought you would be dead by now." I burst out laughing, and he started speaking in his regular tone. Byron was funny and silly. I loved that about him. He didn't even make me feel embarrassed about almost getting my ass beat. We stayed up for hours talking until I fell asleep on him. It seemed to have made him like me more because he called me early the next morning. I told him that I was about to go to the grocery store with my mom and little brother. He begged me to ask my mom to let him go with us. That was new for me, and I honestly wasn't pressed for him to come. I had to explain to him that the incident that he witnessed was child's play compared

Chapter Eight—NEW BEGINNINGS

to how my mom would've reacted If my little brother wasn't with me. Byron was infatuated with me, but he didn't know the complexities of my life. He wanted to spend a lot of time with me like any normal boyfriend would, but I just wasn't ready to be open and exposed in that way yet. It came with too many issues. I'd rather like him and see him in private.

I told him that if he wanted to be bold, I would hand the phone to my mom, and he could ask her. My mom was in the kitchen when I put the phone to her ear. She asked who it was, and I didn't respond. Byron started talking. My mom asked my brother's dad for his opinion. I didn't expect him to say yes, but to my surprise, he told my mom to handle it herself. My mom allowed Byron to go to the store with us. He was so excited. I was indifferent. Byron was in the store rolling the cart with one leg like a big, overgrown kid. He and my little brother were all in the toy section throwing balls. My little brother was the perfect distraction. It was like I wasn't there. On another note, it gave my mom the perfect moment to ask me questions. She wanted to know if I truly liked Byron and, if so, what was the reason. I just assured her that he was just a good friend. She didn't object to that.

I didn't stay enrolled in my new school for a full year. I came home from school one day and our things were put out in the garage and the front of the house. I was flabbergasted. That was the first time I had ever known us to get evicted. The things must have been there a while because the neighbors had alerted people and a car was pulling up ready to thrift when I arrived. My mom popped up from the garage and turned the people away. My mom and I laughed despite the misfortune. Then, she informed me that we were evicted. She said she told the landlord that she'd be out by a certain time, but the landlord just came and put our things outside. I knew it took courage for my mom to tell me that. She was waiting on a guy with a truck to help her move the things before dark. My mom's face was emotionless, but I felt for her. She catered to a lot of people, but when she was in hard times, she was always alone. I don't know if it was by choice because my mom didn't like anyone in her business. Still, I never saw her defeated. She was all about action. I had already had an interesting day at school. My "friend," who I would always sit with on the school bus, traded on me. She changed her appearance and got the girl she wanted. She didn't sit with me that morning or the afternoon, which was unusual. I wasn't bothered until she acted like she didn't even see me in the cafeteria waving at her. I couldn't even process that once I got home and we were evicted. It was Thursday, and my mom asked if I wanted to go to school on Friday. She said that our new house would be ready Monday. She was staying at my brother's dad's house. I asked her if I could stay at Tia's, and I would catch the bus to school. She gave me her permission and instructed me to call her at the end of the school day.

Chapter Nine
LESSONS LEARNED

I was surprised that we moved back to the Westside, and I was transferring back to Douglass High. I was lucky enough to always stay at the same school each time we moved. My little brother was always the one to change schools. We moved to a house near the H.E Holmes train station. My sister came to stay with us until her apartment was ready. My sister and I helped my mom clean and organize. My mom liked things to be put in order quickly. It never took us days for the house to be together. I came to know that Nya had moved too, and she lived right up the street. I invited her and her sisters to come visit me since they wanted to see my sister's pregnant belly. I started visiting Nya every day after school. One day, I was coming from Nya's house when it began to rain. I made it just in time before it started raining heavily. When I walked in the door, my mom and sister were arguing back and forth. "I paid you and now you want me out," I heard my sister yell. I just stood in the living room and peeped around the corner to the room where my sister was standing. "You about to get the fuck out of here," my mom replied. Then, she threatened to call the police. I heard that same line many times before and it hurt my feelings each time.

My sister stormed out of the door right into the storm outside. Luckily for her, the porch was covered, so she didn't get completely soaked. I grabbed the doorknob as my mom was closing the door. "You better get back before you be out there too," she demanded. "Come to the window Adore," my sister suggested. I ran into the room where my little brother was sleeping. "Larry just walked in there," my sister said. I ran out into the hallway and there was my brother's dad walking in my mom's room with her following behind with a plate of food. I went back to the window. My sister asked me to bring her shoes and the rest of her things. I was furious. I hastily passed the shoes and other items out the door. The front door was really close to my mom's room, so I had to be diligent. I went back to the window. My sister said she didn't have any money and had nowhere to go. That enraged me even more. I told my sister to beat on the door, and she did. The only solution I could come up with was to disturb their peace because I knew how important it was to my mom to cater to her man with no distractions. My sister was banging on the screen door loud enough to wake the neighbors! My mom came stomping out of the room. "I'm about to call the police on you. You better get the fuck away from my door." My sister kept banging! The police arrived and spoke with my sister. He said that there wasn't a crime being committed but that my sister would have to leave the porch. My sister left from the porch and all I could think about that night was where she would end up.

As soon as I started going back to my old high school, I got in trouble on my first day. There was a teacher that wasn't familiar to me. Her name was Ms. K, and she was known to be strict. Everyone knew not to play around in her class. I entered her classroom and sat in the front row because I couldn't see. I was laughing and talking to a few of my peers who I hadn't seen since moving away. A few of my classmates were standing in the back row of the classroom talking to me as well. The teacher walked in, and some students started scrambling to their seats. The classroom became quiet. The teacher started talking. "What are the classroom rules once you walk in my door?" She asked. The students replied in unison, "Sit in our seats and put our pencil on the desk and our mouths closed." "So, why were you all up talking then?" she

Chapter Nine—LESSONS LEARNED

responded as she walked to the front of the classroom. The classroom became completely quiet.

I attempted to whisper to the student next to me. I immediately got called out by the teacher, and then everyone knew that I came back on my first day without a pencil. It's not that anyone cared; I just didn't intend to make a bad impression on my new teacher on my first day. "I was just asking for a pencil; it wasn't that deep," I replied. "I think it would be more stupid to sit here without a pencil after you just said all that," I mumbled. The teacher handed me a sharpened pencil and told me to return it before I left class. She rolled her eyes and walked off. I hated that I made such a bad first impression. I wasn't the disruptive type in school. I planned to make it up by being one of the best. Once we were in the hallway transitioning to our next class, two of my classmates were commending me for standing up for myself. They told me that our teacher was rude and strict for no reason. They said they had never seen her "on hush mouth" like that. I just laughed, but that made me feel worse.

My little brother ran into Derrick and his nephew, and they exchanged numbers. I was sitting in the house bored when my brother whispered that Derrick wanted to talk to me on the phone. I hadn't heard from Derrick in a year. I still blushed at the thought of him, though. I talked to him as my brother asked my mom for permission for them to come over. My mom-approved. She rarely told my little brother no. When Derrick asked his mom to drop him off at my house, his mom couldn't believe her ears. She asked him why and then said, "never mind." The funny thing to me was Derrick claimed he was coming to see my brother but told on himself. Derrick and his nephew came over, and Derrick was all in my face. We were in the living room alone. My mom was in her room doing her hair, and my brother was in his room with Derrick's nephew. I had to keep him from trying to stick his hands in my pants. I couldn't believe I wasn't interested in him anymore. I felt like he wasn't on my level. He just wanted sex. My little brother rode with them back to their house, and I stayed home. My mom was still doing her makeup. She said she was taking so long because she was busy making sure Derrick and I weren't doing anything. I laughed because he was definitely trying me.

It was getting late; the doorbell had rung. My mom answered and a white family was on our porch. That was unusual. We had never seen them before, but the daughter knew my brother. The dad was very upset. Supposedly, Derrick's nephew and my little bro were texting their daughter derogatory things and sent a picture of a penis. My mom immediately told me to get on the bus and get my little brother. She said she would pick us up once her friend got there with the car. They sent the text from Derrick's nephew's phone, but it was my brother who offered her number. Once I arrived at Derrick's house, my little brother wasn't there. Derrick's mom was washing a woman's hair in the kitchen sink, but she called the boys for me. She said that I could wait for them in the living room. I sat in the living room and a pregnant girl walked through the door with a family-sized bag of food from checkers. Then, my mom entered. My mom started telling Derrick's mom what the boys had done when she noticed something that I didn't even pay attention to. "Where is Derrick?" My mom asked. "He's back there," his mom answered. She pointed towards the back of the house. Derrick ignored my mom as she beat on his door for him to come out. The pregnant girl was his baby mom, and the lady getting her hair washed was her mom. My mom spoke to Derrick through the door. "How are you going to ignore me when you just left my house with my daughter?" she blasted. Derrick opened the door and the girl's mom came into the living room. My mom continued, "I'm not mad at you; you are young and don't have to commit to anyone." "Just be careful about the things you choose to do," she advised. Derrick's mom shook her head in agreement! I just stood there because I couldn't care less. That was on him. I felt bad for his baby mom. My little brother walked in the front door and my mom slapped him in the head and yelled at him until we made it home. The next morning, I had a friend request on Facebook from Derrick's baby mother.

The timing was terrible to be switching schools. Everyone was preparing for the graduation test. We were expected to pass every subject to graduate high school. We had three chances to pass each subject. The good news was that we could take the test starting from the 11th grade, so if we passed the first time, we didn't have to worry about it our last year. The downside to that was if we didn't pass the one time we took it in the 11th grade, we would have that dark cloud over our heads our last year, plus the stress of passing our senior courses. Something about transitioning from my old environment back to the Westside gave me new confidence. I no longer cared about being the underdog or outcast. I was comfortable in my own skin and my own clothes. I once hated that I was different, but I had finally understood how being different was better. My mom had been preaching that to me for years. I had found myself. I had also started to wear makeup, and I knew how to color my own hair. I wore my hair in a blonde or brown weave. I was feeling myself.

I was never home. It felt good to be back in the city and hanging out with Angel again. When I finally did go home, my mom informed me that we were moving to a house around the corner. The house was on the main street and within walking distance from a park, gas stations, and train station. The house was like our previous house, but there was one big difference. Our previous street was more peaceful. People stood on the block all night near our new house. My mom wasn't expecting that. My little brother already knew most of the people. They weren't familiar with me until we moved on the main street. The guys had been asking my little brother about me, so they started speaking to me every time I walked out of the house. They addressed me by my first name like they knew me. I asked my brother not to talk about me because I didn't want them to know me. My brother was social, so he ended up meeting Tyler. Tyler and I took classes together. Tyler tried to bait my little brother to satisfy his curiosity in knowing if I were sexually active. My 12-year-old brother attempted to defend me by sharing that I only liked Derrick and that none of the guys was my type. Tyler couldn't wait to tell the next day at school. I quickly changed the subject because even a little information was too much.

Despite my brother's efforts in keeping the guys away from me, I started talking to a local drug dealer. He was 21, and his aunt lived around the corner from my house. We started talking when he offered me a ride to the train station. I had seen him around often, so I wasn't afraid to catch a ride from him. I just had to be discreet about it. The walk to the train station wasn't far, so I didn't really need him. I was curious. We kept our relationship low profile. I snuck out of the house a couple times just to sit in his car and listen to music with him. He always took me to the gas station and bought me snacks. We would just park the car and talk. He looked so innocent in the eyes, but he shared wild stories with me of him doing dangerous things. He was never too shelly to compliment me. Once I was sitting in his car eating some munchies and he rested his hand on my thigh. I jumped because I thought he would try me. I spit out my chips when he said, "Girl, nobody trying to get none of that little ass." We never told anyone that we talked, but some people were curious. When he would see me during the day, he would speak to me, but he never stopped me to chat. He would text me in the evening to check on me. He made jokes about

Chapter Nine—LESSONS LEARNED

how I dressed. He said I looked important. When Eric told me he had a daughter, I figured he had a baby mama who was crazy about him somewhere. I didn't want rumors circulating about us, and after I almost got locked out one night, I felt it was time for me to fall back. Besides, my interest was in someone else, a more realistic match for me.

    I was sitting at my desk in reading class when I heard two of my classmates discussing the fine new student. JV was so low-key I didn't know he was in my class for two whole weeks. I looked up from my assignment and asked, "What new student?" The girls signaled me his way. I couldn't see him well enough because I didn't wear my glasses that day, and the lighting in the classroom was too dim. It was time for us to read our journal entries aloud, and I volunteered to go first like I always did. As I was reading, I glimpsed over to get a look at JV. I liked his tawny, brown complexion and nappy temp fade haircut. He had sexy high cheekbones. He had a rough edge about him with gentle eyes. I wanted him and the perfect moment presented itself for me to make my move. Every Friday, we went to the computer lab to study for the graduation test. We had to partner up because there weren't enough computers for everyone. Then, our teacher announced that she needed two groups to stay back and use the classroom computers. I discreetly asked my teacher if I could partner up with the new student, and I'd stay back to help him. She approved. I grabbed his hand and he turned back and grinned at me. JV and I didn't study a thing on the computer, but we learned a lot about each other. He said that all his friends were older, and he transferred from the south side. He told me he had five siblings. I asked him if he noticed me in class, and he replied, "How could I not? You are always the first one to raise your hand to read". I blushed! I asked what he thought of me, and he said I was the cute girl who always read. He was sweet and quiet. I liked the mystery about him. He didn't need to be seen like most boys at the school. We exchanged numbers, and he said he would call me.

The results were in for the graduation test. The intercom came on and the instructions were to go to the auditorium to receive our results. We received a sticker for each subject that we passed & guess what? I failed the math portion. I was disappointed. I didn't even want the stickers. I knew that I had to attend summer school at the end of Summer. I walked to the bus line after getting my results and CeCe and Angel approached me. I told them I passed everything except math. Angel pointed to the stickers on her shirt and commended me for only failing math. CeCe said she passed all subjects too. I wasn't discouraged about not passing; I just dreaded being in school for the summer. I told them I would see them later and got on my bus. The school year may have been over, but Summer was just starting. I was looking forward to starting my first job, and since I failed my graduation test, I had summer school to look forward to as well. The Atlanta Workforce Development Program provided jobs to low-income youth ages 16-21. My sister was working the previous year and swayed me to apply by the deadline. To qualify, candidates had to present a food stamps letter, a transcript or report card, and a form of Identification. I had a couple of weeks before I had to start orientation for my job. I had been hired as a camp counselor at Grant Park Recreation, making $9.25 an hour. I spent most of my time with Angel. We smoked and chilled at her house some days. We had all the snacks since her aunt was the candy lady. We hung out with her cousins some nights, and other nights we went to club Bankhead. Angel's brother was a club promoter, so we'd get in free too.

JV and I had been talking on the phone since the day we exchanged numbers. We never vocally made our relationship official, but we knew we had something together. I purposely didn't sit by him in class because I didn't want people in our business. Ms. Morgan knew we were dating because she saw us hug one another one morning before the bell rang. She just shook her head. Since the other girls didn't know we were together, I was able to peep all of JV's admirers. One of my classmates was always beating on him. She just wanted to brush up on him. One day they both got in trouble and had to separate. JV came and sat by me. I played it cool. We had already discussed the night before that I would come home with him after school.

The day I went home with JV, his mom wasn't there, so I sat downstairs. There was a joke that we had in school, "The only reason some girls meet the parents is that they have to walk past the living room to get to the bedroom." I was determined to make sure that wasn't my story. I intentionally sat downstairs to make my presence known. JV and I just talked as he rested his head on my lap, looking up at me. He told me that I was naturally pretty and kept trying to convince me to go upstairs with him. I stayed on the couch until his grandma came rolling from the room and started yelling at him. His grandma was going on about how he should be ashamed of himself and how he wasn't setting a good example for his little sister. JV defended me. He made it known that it was my idea to meet his family before going to his room, and he commented that I wasn't like that. That made me smile. He knew I was different. I made our relationship official the next day when I texted JV in class and told him to come kiss me when I got the hall pass. He asked me to wait until the bell rang, but I convinced him to do it my way because it would've been too crowded if we had waited. As soon as we kissed, my friend Chasity came out of her classroom and caught us. "That's your boyfriend, Adore?" She asked. "Yep," I replied. When we got back in the classroom, JV said that he didn't know he was my boyfriend. I asked him if it was a problem, and he said that it wasn't; he just didn't know. 11th-grade prom was the following weekend. JV said that he wasn't going. I wasn't going either because I didn't pay my junior fees.

It was Saturday afternoon, the day of prom, and I was chilling at home with my mom and older brother. I had just rodded the ends of my micro twists when Empress pulled up in a red mustang. My brother was the first person to notice. "Ma are you expecting somebody?" he asked. "No," she responded. "It's somebody in a red mustang out there in the driveway." I came walking from the bathroom and my mom came from the kitchen to look out the window. Then, I saw Empress's head perk up from the passenger side with her face all made up. "That's Empress!" I said with excitement. Empress came into the house and told me that I was her date for prom. I told her I didn't pay my dues and I didn't prepare to go. Empress was still set on me going. "I know you have something to wear, and your hair is done," she analyzed. My brother interrupted, "She still didn't pay her dues, though." I asked my bro for some money, and he pulled out two twenties and a ten-dollar bill. Dues were $175, but Empress and I still went to my room and picked out a mini multicolor dress with the shoulder out that I had never worn before. My mom bought the dress from a boutique and decided she didn't want it. I grabbed some blue pumps my mom also gave me. Empress took my rods down, and it was a look. I went to the bathroom and did my makeup. My mom came in and assisted me with the foundation. We stopped by Empress's house. Empress got dressed and we snapped some pictures by the car. We still didn't have a plan as to how I was getting into the prom, but Empress was so positive that I forgot about it. When we entered the front door of the venue, there was a table with four administrators checking names. I became nervous; my palms were sweaty. Empress's name was checked off. Neither of them could find my name. I started looking confused. The coach was one of the administrators and she asked the others to look again as she said, "I'm sure she paid." They didn't find my name. More people were arriving behind us. I whispered to Empress that I would just ride back with her mom. I didn't want to be embarrassed. Empress pulled me to the side and told me to stay calm. She said something I would never forget. She said, "Don't move ahead of God; let God walk in front of you." We walked back up and stood beside her mom. Coach wrote my name down and told me to proceed. Empress and I hugged her mom and walked into the prom. I was so happy that I was able to attend prom and Empress had no idea how she made me feel. I was dancing with my peers when I overheard two of the chaperones discussing me. Both were teachers. The teacher that I didn't know complimented my dress. The other teacher Ms. K, who I thought didn't care for me since my first day in her class, responded, "That is Adore; she always looks nice."

I stayed after school on the last day, and JV was sitting in the computer lab. I just figured he had assignments to make up, but he left at the same time as I did. I asked him what he was working on, and he said he was playing games until I was done. He intentionally stayed after school for me. JV didn't talk much, but he expressed his interest in many ways. I wasn't accustomed to a guy liking me and wanting to spend quality time with me. We walked to the train station and caught the train together. I sat in the seats across from JV, and he waved for me to come sit with him. I didn't care if I seemed weird, but I didn't want him to think I was clingy. After I met his mom, I started coming over more often, and he always wanted me to spend the night. He would look so sad when his mom would say no. One night, his mom wasn't home, and JV wanted me to spend the night. We just had to sneak past his grandma's room to get upstairs. I made it upstairs, but later that night, his grandma came banging on the door, saying she knew I was there. JV and I were so quiet and scared that we tried not to even breathe. We slept in his mom's room and locked the door so she would think that no one was there. That didn't stop her from banging on the door for 20 minutes. "JV, I know you ain't brought that girl in here and took her in your mama room; that's just nasty," she yelled. I had to bury my face in the pillow to prevent myself from laughing out loud. The next morning, we both had to work. JV had gotten a job with the city too. He jumped out the window and came through the front door. He made sure it slammed to see if his grandma was up. His grandma heard it and told him she thought he was upstairs with a girl last night. They talked for a minute and when she turned her back, I eased down the stairs and out the door. JV followed behind me. I called JV on my lunch break, and he informed me that he had gotten fired on his first day. I met him at the train station downtown. He claimed an officer accused him of selling Xanax. I urged him to tell me the truth. He refuted that he really wasn't selling anything. He said he dapped his friend up, and the officer assumed he was making a transaction because of the area. I was disappointed, but I didn't tell him. He said he would find him another job. We hugged, and I headed back to work.

Chapter Ten

CYCLES

It was the last week of school, and my mom told me she had a surprise for me. When I came into the house, she covered my eyes and opened my room door. I had a new bedroom suite. I invited Nya over to see it, and she complimented how nice my mom decorated everything. I caught Nya up on Eric's and my relationship. Nya knew everything about me, but she never told anyone anything. We left my house and smoked on the way to her house. Nya and her sister cooked us wings and let me taste a special sauce that Nya's sister made. I was so high that my eyes were bloodshot red. I borrowed some shades from Nya and went home. I started wearing shades every time I was high from that day forward.

My mom was going on about how my sister needed to do better with her kids and stop taking care of men. I became irritated because I hated how judgmental my mom was about things that she could relate to herself. I told my mom I would be at Angel's house and that I would be going to summer school. Angel drove me to school in her aunt's van my first week, and I caught the Marta bus other times. I stayed at Tia's house on the weekends. One day, my sister called me, and we had regular sister talk. When she let me know that she was running errands for my mom the following Monday concerning Larry, I told her everything that my mom had been saying about her. I told her not to say anything to my mom, but she was so upset that she called and confronted her anyway. My mom called me and cursed me out, telling me to stay out of her business. She told me to stay at Tia's house and don't bring my ass back to her house because I didn't run shit. I should've seen that coming. I told Tia what had happened, and she shook her head. She went downstairs and made us pizza rolls and French fries. We were having a girl talk in her room, and everything was fine between us at first. We were talking about our lives and Tia started crying, saying how she was tired of living in poverty and not having shit. When it was my turn to talk, I explained to Tia that we were not that far in the gutter. I thought I was being uplifting when I told her that she lived in a nice neighborhood and that she was blessed to have a mom who kept her grandkid. I suggested that she get her GED. Tia jumped up, grabbed the box fan, and threw it at me. The fan missed me and hit the window. The loud noise urged Tia's mom to enter the room. "What's going on in here?" she asked. I pointed to the fan and told her mom she threw it at me. Tia started yelling about how I thought I was better than her. Tia's mom suggested that we calm down. Tia stated that she wanted me to leave. "It is 1:00 in the morning, and I am not leaving," I replied. Tia started yelling about how if I didn't leave, she would kill me. She swore on her baby's life. Tia's mom asked me if I could call someone to come get me. I didn't have anyone who would come pick me up that far from my side of town that late. I called Chris. At first, he was reluctant, but when I told him the situation, he asked me where I was going and said he would be there in about 20 minutes. I sat downstairs by the door until he came. I knew I would never speak to Tia again. He dropped me off at Angel's place. The next day, Angel and I were having the time of our lives as usual. I needed some more clothes from home, so I called my mom. It was about 8 pm. She seemed nonchalant when she answered the phone for me, but she approved of me coming to get my things. I alerted her that I would be there in 20 minutes. Or less. She just told me to make sure she got her door key.

Chapter Ten—CYCLES

When I got home. No one was in the house, but the door was unlocked. I quickly went into my room and started grabbing things from the drawers. I also grabbed the book bag that I had organized for my senior year just in case I couldn't come back for the next two weeks. I heard the front door open, so I peeped my head out. It was my little brother. He gave my mom a heads-up that I was there. She was coming into the house behind him. She said, "I don't care," but she continued to my room, grabbed the basket from me, and started walking towards the front door. I was pleading with her not to throw the basket out the door. I wasn't done packing. I told her I would be out in a second. My mom wasn't hearing me. She was babbling about how I talked too much. She was still upset. I was walking behind her when she tossed the basket out the door. All my things inside fell in the grass. My bookbag emptied out as well. That is what infuriated me. She asked me to hand her the door key. I stormed past her onto the porch. "Fuck you!" I yelled. I had never spoken to my mom that way before. My mom slammed the front door on me. I walked over to the empty basket and started gathering my things. I was talking to myself the whole time. I couldn't even finish gathering my things; I was so full of rage. I remembered that I still had the door key. I unlocked the door and flanged it open. My mom swiftly came out of her room. "Adore, give me my key," she demanded. I ran back away from the door. "I'm not giving you shit." My mom slammed the door again. I called my friend, Moses. I had met Moses two summers prior on the Marta Bus on the way to the Six Flags job fair. I didn't get hired, but he did. We became good friends after that. I recalled the events to Moses, and he cautioned me not to do anything that would get me in trouble. I was so mad that I wanted to burn the house down. Moses advised me to take a deep breath and wait on him. He said that he was speeding to me. The more I explained what happened to Moses, the more infuriated I became. Moses hung up without warning. I started pacing back and forth on the lawn. Then, I went back and turned the key in the door. My mom was in the living room. "Little girl, you better gone now," she warned. My mom came out of the house. She jerked at me as if she was going to hit me but didn't. We started walking around each other like in a boxing ring. She jerked at me again. "Bi-," She uttered. Before I knew it, I had punched my mom in the face. I froze in shock, but my mom continued swinging. The next thing I could recall, we were on the ground with people surrounding us. My mom was on top of me; I had my legs wrapped around her. She was reaching for a brick to hit me with. A father and his son were walking down the street near us. The little boy knew my little brother and urged his father to break us up. A voice in the crowd said, "Let them fight ". The little boy responded, "That is mom and daughter." When we were off the ground, my mom still had me by my shirt. "Lil bitch get your weight up," she said as she walked away. I held my tears back because people were watching. Moses was parking his car on the street. I was looking around for my crossbody that was around me and couldn't find it. I saw my braids scattered across the lawn, so I touched the side of my head. I had a bald spot. I started to cry. Moses came and grabbed my things for me. We sat for a while, and I recalled the fight to him. I shared with him that I couldn't find my crossbody bag. My mom appeared in the driver's side window. She tapped on his window, yelling, "get away from my property." Moses became upset and started yelling at my mom about tapping on his window so hard. My mom started cursing him out and calling him names. Moses called the police. I pleaded with him. He circled the block and parked.

 When I spoke with the policeman, I told him that my mom and I wouldn't have fought if she wasn't under the influence and that my friend was the one who called. Moses had already told his story. I told the policeman that I didn't want to press charges and that my friend was just upset. The policeman asked if I knew I was bleeding.

Chapter Ten—CYCLES

I didn't know. The policeman flashed his light on the scratches on the side of my face and neck and called his partner over. They both walked to the door and knocked on the door. My mom didn't answer. The police asked if my mom was in the house, and I said that I wasn't sure. I spent the night at Moses' house and stayed over at Angel's house for school. Angel and Chris were secretly texting. I wouldn't have cared if they would've shown interest in each other. I just didn't understand why they were sneaking. Angel got his number from my phone while I was asleep, and when I turned over, she jumped. I had already caught a glimpse of the number. That is what made the whole interaction a problem. I felt like Angel was being sneaky. When she first met Chris, she shared with me that she felt uncomfortable around him. I stood up for her because Chris was older. I even called him a creep and he stopped talking to me. She conquered and divided us just like that. She started acting weird about Chris, and I just let her be because it wasn't that serious. I wanted her to come out with it at her speed and she did. Well, she told CeCe, and CeCe told me. I finally confronted Angel about her relationship with Chris, and she admitted that she and Chris were becoming a thing. I never scolded her for that, but I told her that we had been friends for too long to let a man break us apart. Chris was originally Tia's friend, so I couldn't feel any type of way, and he didn't stop being there for me.

Angel and I skipped the first day of school. I was reluctant to skip school right after summer vacation, but I was scratched up, and I wasn't in the mood anyway. I didn't understand why Angel wanted to skip. We got dressed and walked to the bus stop so that her older brother wouldn't know we were skipping. We hid until the bus pulled off. We were walking back to her aunt's house when Angel spotted her brother's car coming in our direction. We ran into the nearest yard and hit on the car porch until his car disappeared. When we woke up the next morning, Angel wanted to skip again.

She suggested we skip the whole first week. "We don't get any work the first week anyway," she said. Angel and I were sitting in her room eating snacks when I received a call from my sister. My sister gave word that my mom had been arrested. She said the police picked her up from the house concerning me. I bawled my eyes out as soon as my sister hung up. Angel told me to stop crying so hard or else I could burst a blood vessel in my eye. I started laughing hysterically. Angel comforted me. She said that one day I would get tired of crying, and I would be numb to it like she had become. Then, she asked me to come outside to smoke. I left Angel's house the next morning to hang out with JV. Angel became annoyed with me because I didn't want to get my nails done with her and her mom. She offered to treat me; I just had to meet them at the nail shop. I just didn't feel like bonding with her and her mom. I knew it would only trigger me. I felt responsible for my mom being arrested. Angel became irritated and argued that being under JV too much would only lead him to cheat. I always felt that Angel was kind of clingy, so I didn't pay her any mind. I spent time with JV until someone burglarized my mom's house.

My mom called me from jail, cursing me out and blaming me for her being in jail. I told JV that I needed a break, but we still talked on the phone. I knew that my mom would hold a grudge. My mom had my brother's dad bring him back home with me. I felt safer with my brother in the house. Although my mom had been incarcerated plenty of times before, this was the first time that we lacked anything. Our lights were disconnected, and we were running low on food. I would've called my brother's dad, but he and my mom were feuding. She made it very clear to me to never call him because he would be quick to go take himself off child support. I was feeling hopeless because I didn't want anyone in our business. I was just waiting for my mom to call so she could tell me what to do. My little brother was proactive. He knew almost everyone in the neighborhood and the older men respected him. One of the men in the neighborhood bought us groceries. I woke up one morning and my little brother was bringing groceries in. I got on him about putting people in our business, and he snapped at me, saying that he didn't care because he was hungry. I couldn't argue with him because I was hungry too. My mom called and told me the details to pay the bill.

I dressed in my mom's clothes while she was away. We wore the same size. My school guidance counselor didn't like the way I dressed, so she would forbid me from coming into her office. She cringed at my pencil skirts and bedazzled shirts that had phrases like "kiss me" in the center. She would lecture me about being a young adult entering the workforce. She stressed the importance of appearance and dressing like the job you want. I knew that she'd appreciate my mom's wardrobe. I was called to her office to discuss my senior package so that I knew what was expected of me to graduate. When I stepped into her office, I noticed the subtle pink and green décor. She was a lady of Alpha Kappa Alpha. I was told that I was missing some courses because my credits didn't transfer from my previous school. She explained that I could not move forward without the credits and passing reading and math courses. She informed me that she had requested the scores and was waiting for correspondence. She then talked about my attendance. She was concerned about my missing the first week. My eyes immediately began to water, and she asked me to shut the door so that we could talk. I told her about the fight I had with my mom. I shared with her that I felt trapped in a cycle of bad luck. She comforted me and empowered me. Then, we created a plan. She suggested that I register for credit recovery just in case my credits didn't come back. Next, She suggested I stay after school and take full advantage of the study groups so that I pass the math portion of the graduation test. Then, she advised me to go to the career prep room and sign up to take the SAT right after I was done speaking with her. I had plenty to do in so little time. I still had to pass the current courses I was taking.

    I wanted to attend the field trip to the community college, but I had missed the school bus. I called Eric and he came right away. I wore a black and white pencil skirt and a matching shirt that tied around my neck. When I got in Eric's car, he said I looked like a prostitute, and I called him a hater. He said I knew that he knew that I had a boyfriend because I switched up on him. I laughed it off. I told Eric I had been busy trying to graduate. When we arrived at school, the buses were outside. I kissed Eric on the cheek, and he leaned over in the seat and smacked my butt as I turned around. I dashed towards the building. I didn't know the buses were already loaded. I ran as fast as I could to the buses. I couldn't run too fast because I was busy pulling down my skirt. I caught the bus just in time. I was interested in the fashion design program, so I grabbed some pamphlets. We ate at the food court for lunch. We packed the Chick-fil-A line, and as I was talking to my friend in the line, I heard a familiar voice. I looked up and it was my uncle. I could tell that he was overwhelmed. He was calling out the orders. He was just giving away the food to us. He was like, "What else y'all want?" I tried to still pay for my food, but he told me to go on. I was so happy to see my uncle. I was proud to see my uncle working at a college food court because I knew that he was illiterate. That was the highlight of my day.

    My mom and I engaged in intimate conversation when she came home. She showed me letters that she wrote and shared funny stories with me about some of the women she met. She vowed that we would never fight like that again. She shared with me that she had been reading the bible and came across *Ephesians 6:4*. She acknowledged that she had provoked me, and I admired that. I

Chapter Ten—CYCLES

wasn't expecting my mom to apologize to me or acknowledge her role in our drama. My mom was still recovering her things that were salvaged from the break-in from our neighbor. Our neighbor was the person who discovered that our house was broken into and gathered some of her valuables that weren't stolen. Whoever broke into our house didn't steal any clothes, shoes, or fragrances. When my mom received her clothes, she inquired about her authentic leather jacket. She immediately accused our neighbor of keeping it, and I knew better. I had worn the jacket the day I took the SAT, but I forgot I had hung it on the back of the chair. My mom was upset, so I didn't speak up. I was certain someone had discovered it and kept it. She called our neighbor and argued with her about her jacket. I didn't say anything, and I felt bad. My mom kept repeating the lady's statement about not having the jacket, so I confessed that I had worn it and left it at school. My mom said that I should be ashamed after I watched her curse the lady out. She told me to search for the jacket and not to come home without it. The next morning, I ran to the career center to seek the jacket. The jacket was not on the chair. My heart started racing. I was disappointed, but I didn't panic. My next move was going to be lost and found at the front office. I stood in the middle of the room for a second before I decided to peek in the crack of the tall storage cabinet. There was my mom's jacket hanging up. I was relieved. I put the jacket on and made it to class before the bell rang.

I had so much to do in so little time, and it didn't help that I got kicked out of my math class. My math teacher was Indian and had a strong accent. I didn't understand her and simply asked her to reiterate what she was saying to me, and she pushed me right out the door. Then, she told me I couldn't come back. I was switched to another classroom permanently. My new teacher was a black woman who was all about discipline. She wouldn't even give me a chance in her classroom. All she knew of me was that I was disrespectful to my previous teacher, and she wanted to teach me a lesson. I had a tough time in her class because I couldn't understand her teaching style, and she stopped teaching for the simplest things. She checked anyone who did anything she didn't like at any time. I had failed my math test again for the second time, and I was struggling to pass my senior math class. My math teacher always talked about college prep and was adamant about teaching us "college style" despite most of the class failing the course. I was beginning to feel overwhelmed, and I feared that I would not graduate. At the beginning of the year, everyone was running around happy-go-lucky, but it was mid-semester, and the senior halls were empty before the 1st bell even rang. Everyone was focused. It was crunch time. Senior prom was coming up too. No one was playing around. The afternoon announcements had just gone off, and the halls were full of students when Ms. P, my previous math teacher, stopped me and told me she wanted to help me pass my math test. She said that I was too smart to keep failing. She offered to work with me one on one. Tears filled my eyes and I thanked her immensely. I walked back to her classroom, and we created a study schedule.

I hadn't seen Angel since my mom came home, and I got slumped in my responsibilities, so I asked a dude who rode her school bus if he had seen her. I was stunned by his response. He said I shouldn't have been worried about her because she wasn't a real friend. I told him to shut up and he went on to say, "I asked her about you so I could talk to you, and she called you a bomb and said you be eating at her house and everything." I believed him because Angel came home one day, and she was upset because her aunt gave me the last plate of food. Angel was going on about how it really was for her, but I was there. Then, she said she wasn't tripping about it. Angel and I had been through too much for that to make her angry. I laughed it off and told the guy that Angel wouldn't say that about me. He said, "On God, she did say that." I walked off and headed to the cafeteria and Empress stopped me. Empress pulled me to the side and asked me why Angel was in the classroom with her little sister discussing my business. At first, I didn't see a problem with it because it was Empress's sister, and she was like a little sister to me. Empress had to break it down to me that her little sister wasn't supposed to know my business unless I told her and that she wouldn't even tell my business to her little sister. Then, it made sense to me. Angel was in the classroom telling her business and added me in it to normalize things at my expense. I wasn't sure what Angel had going on, but that was the second time she had my name in her mouth without me being present.

When I was walking out of the cafeteria, I spotted Angel and she looked surprised to see me. She didn't look like herself, though. We spoke to each other, and she said that she had been busy. I confronted her about what the guy told me and about what Empress shared with me. "You believe that junky ass boy, he will tell you anything," she said. I recalled the incident concerning the plate of food at her aunt's house and she still called the guy a liar and said he just wanted me to like him. Then I told her if she chose to tell her business, that is fine, but don't be in the classroom discussing me. Angel said that she would never discuss me with people I'm not cool with, and it was my best friend's sister, so it wasn't a big deal. I expressed to Angel that I don't approve of her sharing stories about me with anyone. Angel got upset and trampled off.

Chapter Eleven
FIGHT OR FLIGHT

I didn't think things would get serious between Angel and me. We were best friends, and we never stayed mad too long, but I was wrong. As the days passed, more things were being revealed to me about Angel that made me question our whole friendship. I had just finished my final attempt of the math portion of the graduation test when one of my peers came to me venting about the test. We were split up all over the campus for the retakes so that none of the rooms were too condensed. As the girl was blabbering on, she disclosed that she and Angel were two of the last four people in their testing area still testing. I looked at her, confused. "Angel?" I asked. "Yeah, she's still in there," she said. "I didn't know she failed math," I mumbled. "She was in Science with me too," the girl added. I was overwhelmed, but I tried to keep a neutral facial expression. The administrator got on the walkie-talkie and alerted the hall monitor that we needed to be escorted back to class. She and I parted ways and couldn't help but think about Angel. I started to think she was acting weird because she was stressed about the tests that she didn't even tell me she failed. How could she consider herself my friend if she didn't even trust me enough to tell me something simple like that? I went back to my classroom, and there was a paper turned face down on my desk. It was a note from my guidance counselor with a list of recommended colleges to apply for. I packed up my things and waited for the bell to ring. I ran into CeCe by the buses. I told her about Angel, and I could tell by the embarrassed look on her face that she knew all along. She decided to confess that Angel didn't pass any of the subjects and that those were her stickers on her shirt junior year. I felt so betrayed and confused. Angel and I spent the whole Summer together partying and doing what I thought was bonding. We even got tattoos together. She drove me to my first day of Summer School. How could she let the whole summer pass by and not tell me? Why didn't she attend summer school?

When I got home, I went straight to my room. I was falling asleep until I received a text notification from JV. He said he missed me. He and I agreed that I would visit him on the weekend. I couldn't wait to see him; it had been a minute. I fell asleep, and when I woke up, I heard Larry's voice. He and my mom were discussing her court date, and she was convincing him that I was going to drop the charges. Larry was just being messy Larry. My mom had already spoken to me about her court date. She told me that her freedom depended on my statement. I didn't need Larry putting things in my mom's head about me. I hadn't even discussed senior prom with my mom. She didn't even ask me about it either. Everyone was talking about prom with so much excitement, but there I was, scared to mention it. I went into my mom's room and sat on her bed. We were engaged in conversation when a commercial about wedding dresses came on the TV. When my mom complimented the dress the model was wearing, I seized the opportunity to mention Prom. The excitement in my mom's voice changed my whole mood. She started talking about hair and makeup. She said that she wanted me in a green dress. I knew that I would look good if my mom had anything to do with it. When I told her that prom was two weeks away, she said that we needed to get going with things. I heard the water from the shower go off, so I walked back to my room. I immediately scheduled my hair appointment. I planned to keep my sewin and just get my hair curled. I didn't even have a date. I texted my big brother how much

Chapter Eleven—FIGHT OR FLIGHT

I had to pay for senior fees, and he said he would come to the school and drop the money off.

It was two weeks until prom and a month until graduation. I had finally passed all the subjects of my graduation test and had just completed my credit recovery course online. The teachers had until the end of the week to turn in final grades. I was headed to my math class when I noticed some of my classmates in the hallway. I asked them what was going on and they let me know that our math teacher quit without turning in our final grades. Everyone was upset, including me. I was under enough stress. Soon as I saw a little light at the end of the tunnel, the cave came closing in. I rushed to my guidance counselor's office in a panic. I pulled out my senior packet to show her all the progress that I had made while I updated her on my teacher quitting. I was stunned when she revealed that my scores had come back from my previous school. I couldn't even be happy about that because I had been in credit recovery all that time in vain. Ms. Sims always kept a calm demeanor. She was already aware that my teacher quit and briefed me that she had registered our entire class for credit recovery. I sighed. I panicked. When I am stressed, I start talking really fast and Ms. Sims caught on to that. "Aww, calm down. You all will be fine," she encouraged. Just as I stepped out of the office, I saw Queen walking towards me in distress. I stepped out of her way and back into the office. Ms. Sims empathized with us and explained that although she wished she could administer us all passing grades, it was not permissible by the board of education.

Queen and I didn't waste any time. We immediately notified our friends and organized a group. We quickly came to know that our questions were not in the same order, but we all had the same questions. The beginning of the course consisted of study material and a few practice questions. We all jotted down our own notes.

The test wasn't timed, so if someone stumbled on a question, they could ask anyone for help. That was our original plan, but of course, we had people who just weren't in favor of the group and did their work and left. Queen and I were the last two to finish. Although we felt the pressure, we helped one another to the end. What was first an unfortunate event turned out to be a bonding experience. My senior packet was complete, and I was officially able to call myself a graduating senior. I was ready for prom. I felt like I deserved it to celebrate. I had been asked by my friend Q to be his date to the prom, and I told him I wanted to wear green. He thought it was perfect. I left the computer lab and walked right into some drama. One of the girls I became close with in math class came to me telling me Angel was jumped. My first instinct was to run to her rescue. I asked her where and who. The girl told me that Angel wasn't my friend. She disclosed to me that Angel told her I didn't have shit and her boyfriend was always buying me things and paying my mom's bills. I knew she was telling the truth because the girl didn't even know the extent to which Angel had me fucked up. I was ready to confront Angel. I walked down to the main office to search for her. When I got to the entrance of the front office, a teacher was also walking in and held the door open for me. Angel was sitting there telling the receptionist what had happened. Before I could think, I yelled, "Bitch, you was never my friend'. The teacher grabbed my arm and pulled me out of the office. She started telling me how she didn't know I could talk like that and how I had too much to lose to fight Angel. Angel was yelling through the door, "Let her in, don't hold her back." My adrenaline was rushing. I was upset. I turned away to head back upstairs and Angel's mom was walking in the front entrance.

    JV had been blowing my phone up with texts and calls but so much was happening, I couldn't focus my attention on any one thing. I finally told him I would come visit him. JV's energy was

Chapter Eleven—FIGHT OR FLIGHT

different. He was his usual affectionate self, but the energy in the room felt heavy. I started wrestling with JV to lighten the mood. He grabbed me, turned me on my back, and kissed my forehead. Then, he said we needed to talk. I sat up on the bed next to him, and he looked at me and said, "I didn't cheat on you." "But what?" I replied. JV told me he had a baby on the way. I couldn't believe what I was hearing. "JV, you couldn't hold me down for two months?" "You knew everything I was going through." JV stated that this was something that had happened before us. He went on to say he and the girl were never together; they just slept around a few times. He claimed the girl had a boyfriend, so the baby may not be his. JV and I were only dating for about 9 months or less, but we had experienced real-life situations together. I cheated on JV over the Summer, and he forgave me. I knew JV to be genuine; he wasn't spiteful. I was hurt so, I had to leave. When I got home, I was relieved that my mom wasn't home. I felt suffocated the whole bus ride. Everything hit me at once. It wasn't until I looked at the mirror that the tears came flowing down. I saw the pain in my own eyes. I started crying so hard that I started hyperventilating. I didn't know when my mom would walk into the house, so I ran the bath water. I ended up turning it off and lying on my bed. When I woke up, I fixed myself a plate of food. I was so sad when I came home, I didn't even notice my mom had cooked for me.

I sat on my bed and opened the Facebook app. One of my Facebook friends had written a post congratulating JV and his baby mom on becoming parents to be. I didn't even know I followed her. That let me know that his baby mom knew of me and had her friend follow me. I searched through her, JV, and his baby mom's Facebook profiles to see what I missed. JV and his baby mom had history. I didn't want to be involved anymore. I was familiar with that kind of drama. I didn't want it and I didn't need it. I blocked JV's number.

I got my hair curled two days before prom because that was the only available appointment. By the time I ran around to get my nails done and went dress shopping, my hair needed a refresher. My mom said that she knew a shop where I could go, and I could just walk in. She said the lady was good with curls as she did her hair back in the day. I trusted my mom's judgment, and I was desperate. No one else was available to fix my hair the day of prom. I knew that a lot of people admired my mom, and I was certain they knew not to mess me up. When we arrived at the shop, I noticed that other girls were getting their hair ready for prom too. The beautician washed my hair, added rollers, and set me under the dryer. When I was done under the dryer, she started to style my hair. In the corner of my eye, I caught a glimpse of the beautician dipping her hand in the black Ampro gel. She put it on my edges. I felt her stroking the brush in a swooping motion as if to swoop my sides. She added the black strips and began to curl my hair. I wanted my hair in soft curls, that's it. When she sprayed lots of spritz on my curls, I felt uneasy but didn't say anything. I wasn't familiar with her method, but I was trusting the process. She started teasing my curls, and that is how I knew she was nearly finished. The other beauticians were complimenting the other girls in the shop, but not me. She handed me the mirror and I wanted to do one of those loud screams where all the windows break. Everything my mom said started to make sense. She probably did do my mom's hair back in the day because she was clearly not with the times. I looked like Shirley Chisolm and she mishandled my Brazilian bundles. "I like it," I screeched. Q walked in just in time. He wanted to bring me breakfast. He didn't say anything about my hair; he just handed me my food and said he would see me later. I walked outside to call my mom. She came as soon as possible and I started telling her how she told me to go to that lady and how much she ruined my day. My mom and I were arguing back and forth until I told her I wasn't attending prom anymore. She said she didn't care but continued to call everyone on her contact list to help me. Finally, my brother's wife had come to save the day. She came over to my mom's house and after a glimpse at my hair, she uttered, "I see why Adore is distraught; that lady fucked her up." She took me to her friend's shop. I had the royal treatment. When the beautician washed my hair, my sew-in was loose, so we ended up taking the whole thing out. She reused some of the bundles and added a few colored pieces from her drawer. She gave me a nice ponytail with a swoop. I drank a wine cooler while I got my makeup done and when I saw myself, I felt pretty. I was back in the mood for prom.

When we pulled back up to my mom's house, it was dark outside, and the street was full of cars like there was a party. My mom had bamboo torch lights sticking out of the ground. As I walked closer, I heard music from the inside. I opened the front door and some of my family members were hanging out. It became apparent to me that my mom orchestrated a party for me. Prom was the next hour, so I had no time to mingle before my mom hauled me away. My grandmother was in my room drinking a wine cooler. She and my mom helped me get dressed. I kissed my mom on her face and told her thank you. I felt so special. We walked out of the room, and Q was there conversing with my family. We walked outside to take pictures by the light when my mom asked Q about the car we were driving. Q pointed to the minivan, and my mom threw a fit. My sister-in-law and I burst into laughter because we thought the minivan was cool. My mom called my big brother and told him to bring me a car because she didn't want me pulling up in a minivan. Q explained that after prom, we were going to eat with some friends and the van would fit all of us. My mom suggested he drive the minivan by himself while I followed him in the car, and we could drive back in the minivan. By the time we sorted out the car situation, we were late for prom. When we arrived, no one even saw us pull up. We did still go out to eat after prom, and Q got me home right before midnight. The last week of school was dedicated to graduation practice, and I brought my camera to take pictures of everyone. I also asked a few of my teachers for college recommendation letters as I was completing my college applications. I decided to ask Ms. K, and she was excited to help me. She asked me for the name and addresses of the schools to which I was applying. She said that she would have the letter by the end of the day. When I asked Ms. K. what she put into the letter, she said she wasn't telling me with a smile on her face.

We received 10 invitations to graduation, but I only needed two. My mom and big brother were the only people I expected to come to my graduation. Chris called and asked me for an invitation, and I was more than happy to give him one. He said he had been asking Angel, but every time he was on the way to pick it up, she was always busy. I gave him the time to come get his invitation and he came right away. He congratulated me and told me he would be at my graduation to support me. After graduation practice, I received a call from Angel. She had the nerve to confront me about giving Chris an invitation and to add that she had already spoken with him and demanded that he stop communicating with me. I told Angel that she was the only one losing, and Chris would be in my life until I decided to change things. Then, I hung up in her face and blocked her number.

We were lining up to walk across the stage when I spotted my math teacher; the one who neglected our entire class had a front-row seat. Everyone was whispering about him. He was bold to show up, but it made our walk even more victorious. I didn't expect to cry at my graduation, but once I received my diploma, I looked around and realized that I would miss those people. I hugged Ms. Morgan and she consoled me. She whispered, "You will be fine," and patted me on the back. After taking pictures with my family,

Chapter Eleven—FIGHT OR FLIGHT

we drove off and my brother played "You deserve it" by future. Those lyrics spoke to my soul. We pulled up to the gas station, and I received a call from a private number. It was Angel. "I told you not to give my nigga an invitation bitch," she yelled through the phone. I put her on speaker, and my mom gave me a confused look. I replied, "This Angel." "Tell her to come on. She knows where we are," my mom replied. My brother laughed. My mom and brother had no idea what transpired between Angel and me, and I wasn't in the mood to tell the whole story.

I was a camp counselor at my first job working with the Atlanta Workforce Development Program, but this time I was chosen to intern with the Department of Community Development in the City Hall building. I mostly just handled mail and ran errands for the employees, but I felt fortunate just to have the opportunity to be amongst the professionals. I did learn professional etiquette and received resume assistance. I also attended meetings. When we would have gatherings, they would let me take the remainder of the food home, but I never did. I would give the food to the homeless community on my walk to the 5-points train station. I made connections with my supervisors and was offered a permanent position as a receptionist in that department until I informed them that I was accepted into college.

I came home from work one day and my mom brought me the letter. I had applied for three colleges, but Talladega College responded first. I was super excited because I was told that it was "The Harvard of the South." I ran into my mom's room and called my big brother because he said if I went to college, he would buy me a car. When I told my coworkers about attending college, they planned a gathering, gave me their business cards, and brought me gifts. For a second, I wanted to take the opportunity, but I thought about the future. If I graduated college, I'd be the first in my family.

I would set the standard for the generation after me. I would be a generational curse breaker. I would have opportunities to live my dreams. I would rise above poverty.

My sister moved into her first apartment, so I had been sleeping over often. I wanted to spend as much time as possible with my niece and nephews. My niece and I were really close, so I spent most of my time with her. My mom and sister were at odds again, and I didn't want to be involved, but my mom still added me to the confusion. She started accusing my sister of taking me away from her and saying that my sister was a bad influence. Then, she would call me and tell me I needed to stay away from my sister's apartment because no one was doing anything positive there, and I would end up being complacent. I simply explained to my mom that I had my own mind and had chosen to be at my sister's place. I wasn't forced. My sister's apartments were in the projects, but she lived right in the front, so I didn't have the concern of being in the middle of any mess. Something was always happening, but I stayed in the house while I was there. I didn't even want to be a witness to anything. The thing about my mom was that she made a lot of sense most of the time, but her intentions weren't pure. My mom was concerned about my sister charging me to stay at her place, but she was going to do the same thing. There were pros and cons in both situations. I had my own physical space at my mom's house, but I didn't have my own mental space. My sister's house was noisier and more populated, but I didn't have the anxiety of worrying about one disagreement being blown out of proportion.

I met a guy and we started dating. I had been sitting on the porch one night when he came and gave me his number. I didn't call him. He was dark-skinned, tall, with locs. His soft baby hairs around his locs made them look good even though he obviously hadn't had a retwist for some time. He didn't dress like most guys in the hood

Chapter Eleven—FIGHT OR FLIGHT

either. He had on a button-down shirt and khakis like he had just come from work. I noticed him, but I still didn't want to know him. I was fixing some ramen noodles when he walked in and confronted me about not using his number. He said he heard great things about me and wanted me to know he didn't live in the apartments. He let me know that his aunt and cousins lived in the community, and he just visited them sometimes. My sister had already given me a word about him, but I listened to him. He was attractive and seemed to have business about himself, so I gave him a chance. I only had a month left before I would leave for school.

Dee and I hit off quickly. On his 21st birthday, he took me out to a club in midtown. We were partying with the white folks. He liked to have fun and drink. I wasn't old enough to drink, but the white guys were buying us both drinks. Dee was fun. He dared me to dance with this gay couple, and I did. Then, he got jealous and said he didn't ask me to be all in a sandwich with them. We were so drunk; we were holding each other up leaving the club. He stayed in the apartments all night. He would come and get me off my sister's sofa at 3 am in the morning sometimes. He would take me home with him. He lived with his mom and little sister. I became acquainted with them, and they liked me, especially his mom. She commended me on going to college and shared stories with me about Dee and herself. Dee and I were freaking like it was going out of style and he could cook. When we stayed at his place, he cooked me breakfast before we left. I liked being at his house, and I didn't understand why he enjoyed being in the apartments. He had a nice home. My sister's boyfriend was the one to tell me that Dee had a drinking problem, but I was already figuring it out. Dee's aunt and my sister hooked us up but neglected to tell me about that. I couldn't get deep into that, though, because it was time for me to go. Before I left, I wanted to get one more tattoo, and I had to get my hair braided. Dee had been calling me all day, but I was busy. Although I worked over the Summer, I blew most of my money on weaves and tattoos, and I paid my sister. My big brother bought all of the things I needed for school, and he was the one driving me to school. It was the night before my departure, and my big brother was on the way to get me when Dee came over drunk, kissing all on me. I was feeling anxious in the bathroom, packing up my flat irons. I couldn't focus on Dee and really wanted him to be gone when my big brother pulled up. I looked back and Dee was sitting on the edge of the tub crying. I started laughing, and he started yelling at me, calling me insensitive. "You're really leaving me, and you think this shit funny," he cried. "Dee, you knew I was leaving for College this whole time, so what am I supposed to do?" I responded. Dee grabbed both of my shoulders and told me how much he would miss me and to call him when I made it. The next morning my brother and I organized my things and stopped at my mom's house.

My mom hugged me tight and started pulling out articles of clothing from her drawers and closet. She said that she would mail me her food stamps card and instructed me to call her if I needed anything. I hugged her tight, and I was off to school.

ABOUT THE AUTHOR

Daphne Jackson is a mother, Licensed Social Worker, and trail blazer originating from Atlanta, Georgia. Her love for reading and storytelling began as early as age two. Daphne recalls in her early years saying she would be an author, "When she grows up". That dream revisited her in 2018 when she found herself writing, "Best Seller" on her vision board without even having written a book. In 2019 she began to create, Too Phased. Daphne is no stranger to adversity and believes that advocacy changes lives. Through articulate storytelling, she unmasks some of the cycles, barriers, guidance, and decisions that impacts generations. She conjoins controversial topics with real life experiences

www.ingramcontent.com/pod-product-compliance
Lightning Source LLC
Chambersburg PA
CBHW050912160426
43194CB00011B/2376